If you watch the ads on television, you'll see that we place a high priority on "feeling just right." There's a drug for virtually every physical pain, every emotional disturbance.

If you feel down, take "uppers"; if you're emotionally excitable, take "downers." If you have a sexual urge, fulfill it; if you have anger express it; if you feel tied down, walk away from your responsibilities. It's your life and you're number one, so do as you please.

But as Erwin Lutzer will show you, blindly following your feelings is not the path to happiness.

MANAGING YOUR EMOTIONS

MANAGING YOUR EMOTIONS

Erwin Lutzer

This book is designed for your reading pleasure and profit. It is also designed for group study. A leader's guide with helps and hints for teachers and visual aids (Victor Multiuse Transparency Masters) is available from your local bookstore or from the publisher.

VICTOR BOOKS ®
A DIVISION OF SCRIPTURE PRESS PUBLICATIONS INC.
USA CANADA ENGLAND

Seventh printing, 1988

Unless otherwise noted, Scripture quotations are from the *New American Standard Bible*, © the Lockman Foundation 1960, 1962, 1963, 1968, 1971, 1972, 1973, 1975, 1977. Other quotations are from the *Holy Bible, New International Version* (NIV), © 1973, 1978, 1984, International Bible Society. Used by permission of Zondervan Bible Publishers and the *King James Version* (KJV). Used by permission.

Recommended Dewey Decimal Classification: 248.4
Suggested Subject Headings: EMOTIONS; FEELINGS

Library of Congress Catalog Card Number: 82-62435
ISBN: 0-88207-386-9

© 1983 by SP Publications, Inc. All rights reserved
Printed in the United States of America

VICTOR BOOKS
A division of SP Publications, Inc.
Wheaton, Illinoios 60187

Contents

Preface

GOD created us with emotions so that we might be able to enjoy Him and His creation. Often we have been tempted to consider our feelings as a bother, a hindrance to living a life of faith. Although it is true that as fallen creatures our emotions often lead us astray, we must remember that God gave us emotions so that we might live a well-balanced and wholesome life. After all, God Himself is an emotional being who expresses anger, pleasure, and compassion. Our goal, then, ought not to be to suppress our emotions, but rather to achieve emotional wholeness through finding God's answers for our emotional needs. If those who read this book should be helped along the road to emotional stability, my efforts will be well rewarded.

I'm indebted to many people who have helped shape my thinking about emotions: Jay Adams, James Dobson, and David Augsburger come immediately to mind. Also, I'd like to express a special word of appreciation to my pastor, Richard Sipley, for his provocative thoughts regarding the problems of human emotions. His insights are particularly reflected in my chapters on love and fear.

I wish to thank my good friend, Mr. Les Stobbe, for his encouragement and editorial assistance. And I am especially appreciative of my secretary, Terri Ambrulavich, who typed the manuscript. Finally, I am grateful to the people of the Moody Church, who have given me the privilege of sharing the fruits of my study with them.

ERWIN W. LUTZER

To the memory of my nephew, Dallas, whose untimely death introduced us to the emotion of sorrow.

1

Learning to Cope

EMOTIONS. What should we do with them?

Though some might feel that God was rather stingy in bestowing some of His gifts, we would all agree that He was generous when He gave us emotions. We all have experienced so many passions and feelings that, as one person has correctly said, we are millionaires in emotions—they come in infinite combinations of types and intensities. Just as we may experience physical pain or pleasure, so we have the capacity to experience emotional pain or pleasure.

Unfortunately, we usually think of our feelings in negative terms. We're so accustomed to hearing the phrase "emotional problems" that we think our emotions are a bother. No doubt many of us have sometimes thought that we'd be better off without them.

As a result, we often try to ignore our emotions. This seems to be a popular approach taken by many Christian writers who see our emotional makeup as a hindrance to spiritual progress. We've had the impression that our emotions are an embarrassment to us—an unwanted appendage.

For example, we're probably all acquainted with the fact, faith, and feeling trilogy. We are told that our forgiveness is based on facts, namely, the death and resurrection of Jesus Christ. We must exercise faith in these facts, and then our feelings will eventually follow suit. At any rate, our feelings must be ignored; they are a hindrance to living lives of pure faith.

I agree with this analysis, at least to some extent. Yes, feelings can lead us astray; yes, we must believe the facts of the Gospel, regardless of the emotional turbulence we may experience. But are our emotions an enemy of Christian growth and maturity?

To say that we should believe facts and ignore feelings invites us to deny our feelings. It encourages us to suppress our negative emotions rather than benefit from them. Husbands have often developed insensitivity toward their wives by simply repeating what they have heard in church—that your feelings should be rejected. Yet those feelings are important. They are a part of our total being.

I've known angry people who deny their anger; they are unable to admit such feelings, believing that such an admission would be tantamount to a confession of spiritual carnality. Others deny hostility, bitterness, or sorrow. Thinking that Christians should not have such feelings, they insist that they are free from them. The result is that deep feelings often smolder beneath the surface of their personalities. I am convinced that emotional wholeness cannot be achieved through denying the deep emotions that we all have.

Some people have allowed the pendulum to swing in the opposite direction. They have made their feelings the focus of their attention. Our nation has become steeped in sensuality (i.e., the belief that we should be motivated by our senses). Watch the ads on television and you'll soon learn that we have placed a high priority on "feeling just right." There is a drug for virtually every physical pain, every emotional disturbance. If you feel down, take "uppers"; if you're emotionally excitable, take "downers." But at all costs, feel good!

Much of modern psychology has contributed to this focus of our pleasure-seeking generation. For one thing, modern man believes he has evolved from lower forms of life, which means he is made up solely of *matter*—he has no immaterial substance, such as a soul or a spirit. Therefore, all human feelings are only physical or chemical reactions. The conclusion is that all emotional disorders have a chemical cause. Since nothing can ever be wrong with me spiritually, there can only be physical disorders, and these can be cured with drugs.

Also, secular psychology, cut loose from moral absolutes, is incapable of judging behavior. Thus, we can understand why people would conclude that they can do whatever they feel like doing. If you have a sexual urge, fulfill it; if you have anger, express it; if you feel tied down, walk away from your responsibilities. At any rate, it's your life and you're number one, so do as you please.

But following your feelings, doing whatever your animal urges dictate, is the surest way to a life of spiritual ruin. All of us were born with a sinful nature that wants its desires fulfilled. And though our feelings in themselves may not be sinful, fulfilling them without the instruction of Scripture and the power of the Holy Spirit would be disastrous. Michel Quoist has said, "Emotions and physical desires are like headstrong steeds . . . . You have to keep the reins firmly in hand" (*The Christian Response*, Fides). Blindly following your feelings is not the path to happiness.

Between these two extremes lies the biblical balance based on the following truths:

1. *God the Creator has emotions and therefore endowed us, who are created in His image, with similar emotional capacities.* Throughout the history of the church, theologians, and

particularly philosophers, have denied that God has feelings. Apparently, it was believed that such an admission would demean the concept of an immutable God. For instance, the Westminster Confession of Faith states, "There is but one only living and true God who is . . . without body, parts or *passions*" (author's italics, II 1, 1648). But the Scriptures teach otherwise: "And the Lord was sorry that He had made man on the earth, and He was grieved in His heart" (Gen. 6:6). God became weary of hypocrisy (Isa. 1:11-14), and of course His anger against sin is expressed numerous times throughout the Bible.

Look at Christ, who displayed the divine nature. He expressed sorrow (John 11:35), anger (Mark 3:5), frustration (Luke 9:41), amazement (Luke 7:9), and joy (Heb. 12:2). Thus, to deny our emotions, to be unwilling to admit our anger, is to be unprepared to do what God Himself does, namely, to affirm that He is indeed angry with the wicked. Our emotional makeup is but one of the ways by which the image of God is seen in us.

2. *Man created in the image of God is a physical, spiritual, and emotional unity.* With our bodies we can relate to our physical environment, with our spirits we can be in fellowship with God, and with our emotions we can be affected by either relationship. In fact, we sometimes cannot easily separate the various aspects of man in common experience. When we act or react to circumstances, we are intricate, unified,. and mysterious beings. As a result, our emotions can be affected by our relationship with God or the haphazard and fluctuating experiences of life.

One day a two-year-old child wanders away from home and is lost for several hours. The parents, neighbors, and police search frantically, but without success. Two other children were kidnapped in the area within the last year. The child's parents are filled with regret ("Why did we let him play alone in the front yard?"), anger ("Who would do such an awful thing?"), and fear ("How can we cope in the days ahead?"). But just before sundown, the child is found sleeping peacefully in a neighbor's garden. Imagine the elation when the parents discovered that all their turbulent emotions were unfounded. Think of the relief, satisfaction, and joy when the boy has had his supper and is tucked into bed that evening.

Now visualize an entirely different scene. A woman filled with depression has already put the sleeping pills in her purse. This will be her last day on earth. But before she swallows the contents of that small bottle, she makes one last stop at a friend's house; it will be her way of saying good-bye. To her surprise, she finds several women gathered in the home for a Bible study. The depressed woman is invited to stay, and she does so reluctantly, thinking this will be her last time to give God—if He exists—a chance. After the study, she lingers to ask some questions: "Can God do something for me?" An hour later, she realizes that it was the guilt from an ongoing illicit sexual relationship she was having that was the cause of her depression. She accepts Christ's forgiveness for her sin, and suddenly the heavy sense of guilt and depression is gone. The bottle of pills lies unopened in her purse as she leaves for home—lighthearted, free, and clean.

These true stories remind us that our emotions can be deeply affected by either our circumstances or our relationships with God. Physical illness affects our emotional equilibrium. And the reverse is also true: our emotions can affect our physical health. Many diseases are considered psychosomatic; the physical ailment is caused by emotional disorders. For example, we cannot live with guilt without having it affect our bodies. Anger exacts an enormous physical penalty—it can cause everything from ulcers to backaches. I read recently that heart attacks are more often caused by emotional stress than lack of exercise. The consequences of emotional disorders are built right into the basic fabric of human life. We can talk about our body, soul, and spirit for the purpose of analysis, but we live, breathe, and react as one entity, a unity.

3. *God created us with emotions so that our lives might be enriched.* God could have created us without emotions; we could be intelligent, calculating, insensitive machines. But life would be exceedingly dull. True, there would be no sorrow, but there would be no joy either. We would live without a sense of anticipation, and we would not experience the comfort that can be ours at a time of tragedy. Life would progress without the laughter of children, without the spontaneity of lovers, or without the sympathy of friends. But God is not like that, nor did He wish us to be. Our emotions were given not to control us, but that we might be able to enjoy life. We would *not* be better off if we were free of them.

4. *God's primary means of bringing about our emotional healing is by working through our spirits rather than adjusting our physical or environmental circumstances. Consequently, our negative emotions such as bitterness, rejection, and anger are not to be ignored.* Just as bodily pain is God's way of telling us that something has gone awry with our physical nature, so emotional pain may tell us that all is not well with our spiritual nature. And if we try to solve a spiritual problem with a physical remedy (such as curing depression with drugs), the results will be disappointing.

It's popular to think that the answer to our spiritual needs is a physical stimulus. In a shopping mall, I overheard a salesclerk say to a customer, "You owe it to yourself to get these cosmetics. All of us are in the dumps once in a while, and we deserve to make ourselves happy. If the people around you don't make you happy, then it's up to you to make yourself happy." If the customer accepted this advice and did indeed feel better because of her improved appearance, she would be greatly mistaken to interpret that improvement as the answer to life's doldrums. A physical remedy can at times appear to solve a spiritual problem, but it can only camouflage the real source of trouble. Our spiritual and emotional natures must ultimately be brought into harmony with God. Only then can we achieve emotional balance. Remember Augustine's words: "O Lord, Thou has made us for Thyself and our hearts are restless until they find their all in Thee."

I'm not saying that all emotional disorders have spiritual causes. Our physical conditions can affect our emotional stability; drugs can cause emotional disturbances that can be either detrimental or beneficial. But God's desire for each person is emotional and spiritual wholeness; *He wants our emotional stability to be based on our relationship with Him rather than on physical or chemical stimuli.*

What, then, should we do with our emotions? The answer is to (1) admit to ourselves and to God how we feel (sometimes we should admit our feelings to others too) and (2) ask ourselves: Why do I feel the way I do? The answer to this question is often difficult and sometimes impossible to give. We've all felt like David, who asked himself, "Why are you in despair, O my soul? And why have you become disturbed within me?" (Ps. 42:5) But more importantly, we must (3) find out what the Bible teaches so that we will have divine direction on managing our fluctuating feelings.

Then, (4) we must realize that emotional wholeness follows obedience and not vice versa. Many people do not obey God's Word because they think they must *feel* like it; that is, they think that unless they obey with emotional exhilaration, they are guilty of hypocrisy.

Not true. No doubt Christ did not feel like going to the cross; the thought did not give Him emotional pleasure. Yet in the end He experienced the emotional satisfaction of joy (Heb. 12:2). The joy followed obedience; it did not precede it.

Application

1. Write down all the emotions you have experienced within the past week. Can you remember what caused the fluctuation in those feelings? Circumstances? Your relationship with God? Your health?

2. Read the Gospels, looking for clues regarding the emotions Christ felt when He was here on earth. Here are a few passages to get you started Matthew 9:36; 26:36-46; 27:46; Mark 3:5; Luke 24:25; John 11:35; 12:27-28.

3. Study the nine aspects of the fruit of the Spirit (Gal. 5:22-23), and highlight those that directly influence our emotions.

4. Discuss: In what ways do we often deny our emotions—or suppress them rather than facing them and then doing something about them?

5. God expects us to have a feeling of compassion. What sins dull our sensitivity to human need? (See Eph. 4:17-24.)

6. What emotions do you want God to help you control? List ways to face those feelings so that they might be made subject to Christ.

2

Steps to Emotional Wholeness

WHILE driving from Dallas to Chicago, my wife and I stopped at a restaurant for dinner. Moments later, a woman and her three-year-old daughter came and sat at the table next to us. We exchanged pleasantries, and our own children spoke with the little girl, who sat close to her mother.

Fifteen minutes later, a man walked in and sat beside the woman, and a conversation ensued. From bits and pieces of the discussion, we put the story together: they'd been divorced and had agreed to meet there to transfer their daughter from one to the other. The little girl listened as her parents talked and argued in her presence. They disagreed regarding the amount of money that had been paid for alimony, and the matter was left unresolved. Then the father left with his daughter walking beside him. She waved good-bye to her mother, and together they walked into the night.

Think of what this three-year-old girl faces: she is to love her mommy during the week and her daddy on weekends. But her mommy and daddy don't love each other; they can't be together for five minutes without arguing. She's supposed to feel secure even though her

21

daddy has found someone more exciting than her mommy to live with. She'll have to adjust to her "new" mommy too. Meanwhile, she is transferred from one to the other like a package; she doubtless thinks she is a bother, a nuisance to these adults who gave her physical life.

This girl represents millions of children who are either unloved or think they are unloved because of the breakup of the family. More than one-half of all the children born today will, at some time, live with a single parent. Add to this the estimated 2 million children who are physically abused and we readily see that the emotional consequences are immense. We are already reaping the harvest—millions of people experience depression, rejection, frustration, and guilt. Yet, I think we've seen only the tip of an iceberg; the consequences will escalate from generation to generation.

At the risk of oversimplification, let me suggest some basic steps needed in emotional healing. I'm not saying that their application is simple; in most instances, it takes time to overcome the hurts of the past. But God has not left us without resources in our quest for emotional wholeness. Christ is well able to heal the brokenhearted.

1. *The past must be forgiven by God, and we must be cleansed from its influence.* Later, I shall explain more fully the need for both forgiveness and cleansing. At this point, let's define the difference. Forgiveness is God's gift to us that assures us of a right standing in His presence. Cleansing is the application of forgiveness to us directly. It is important that the past be put behind us, both legally and in experience.

Some people speak about the need for the healing of memories. My wife attended a seminar led by a person who had a woman from the audience recount in detail her sexual experience with her grandfather. The purpose was that this woman might be able to think of Christ during the experience and put the emotional trauma of that event behind her. Though I can appreciate the goal of such therapy, I question its biblical validity.

There is an emphasis in the Scriptures, however, on the renewing of the mind. I believe that God is able to heal our memories. That does not mean that we will never think of the unpleasant experiences of the past, but they need not become the focus of our attention. I've spoken to people who can recall only with great difficulty some of the crushing experiences they have had because God has renewed their minds. The present and the future occupy their attention, and their past no longer has control over them.

The Apostle Paul alluded to this in Ephesians 4:19, where he told us that many people have given themselves over to sensuality and impurity. Then he talked about our life without God, the corruption and the control of lusts that are latent within us all. But then he urged us to be "renewed in the spirit of your mind, and put on the new self, which in the likeness of God has been created in righteousness and holiness of the truth" (vv. 23-24). The renewed mind is different from the natural mind, which focuses on negative emotions rather than the positive light of the Gospel.

We all know it is God's will that Christ be formed in us, that we be changed into His likeness. We are to be "conformed to the image of His Son" (Rom. 8:29). God does not want us to be chained to the hurts of the past, as such enslavement would hinder Christlikeness. He forgives us and then cleanses our minds from the ill effects of the rejection and guilt that we may carry with us. I'm not saying that such deliverance will take place speedily, though I have known those who have had instant deliverance from the harassment of memories. But if we stand our ground, there will be emotional release.

More specifically, the blotting out of our past necessitates clarifying erroneous concepts. For example, many people have wrong notions of God that make them afraid of Him rather than perceiving Him as a God of acceptance and love. So a foundation must be laid to help people with destructive emotions. Or consider a person who has grown up in a home in which sex was considered sinful even within prescribed biblical limits. Such a person may grow up and marry, only to learn that he or she cannot relate sexually to a marriage partner. Here again, there must be clarification that will enable the person to be freed from childhood inhibitions. The cleansing we have talked about must take place within the context of biblical teaching so that the mind can be filled with God's perspective.

Only when we choose to forgive those who have wronged us can we expect that the bitterness and the emotional hurt will begin to subside. Forgiveness is something we do for others, but we also do it for our own good. It's part of the process of wiping out a hurtful past.

2. *We must exalt the Cross as God's answer to emotional hurts.* Usually when we think of Christ's work on the Cross, we emphasize that He died in our stead that we might be freed from sin. What is less known is that the same death took place that we might have emotional freedom. In Isaiah 53:4, we learn that Christ identified Himself with our feelings: "Surely our griefs He Himself bore, and our sorrows He carried." Isaiah predicted that the Spirit of the Lord would come upon Christ and anoint Him "to bring good news to the afflicted; He has sent me to bind up the brokenhearted, to proclaim liberty to captives, and freedom to prisoners" (Isa. 61:1). Just as the Cross represents an exchange for our sin—our sin is imputed to Christ and His righteousness is imputed to us—so it is with our emotional responses. As we commit ourselves to Him, He brings about emotional wholeness so that we might be able to live out His life in us.

I'm not implying that we should expect to live in perpetual emotional tranquility, for Christ Himself experienced grief, sorrow, rejection, and depression. But He was able to endure them because of the triumph of His obedience. Paul explained that redemption was accomplished for the body, soul, and spirit. And though total deliverance will only take place when we are in heaven, we can begin to benefit from that redemption *now*. The Cross includes deliverance from emotional slavery.

Think of it this way: suppose you lived in an apartment complex in which the landlord harassed you, charging exorbitant rent and blackmailing you. You became filled with fear, anxiety, guilt, and depression. Yet there was nothing you could do, for you were captive to this intruder. But suppose that a new landlord buys the apartment complex. He is kind and considerate, and rather than using intimidation, he lavishes you with love. Now what if your former landlord returned and demanded your allegiance once again? You'd tell him to take up the matter with the new landlord and then firmly shut the door! That's what Christ has given us the authority to do, because we as believers are under new management. The taxing emotional burdens of the past need no longer be carried by us, for we have a new owner. And when He said, "You shall know the truth, and the truth shall make you free" (John 8:32), that freedom included release from emotional slavery. Because of the Cross, no feelings need rule over us.

3. *The body of Christ must provide a strong emotional acceptance.* Yes, God accepts us, but He also wants His people to demonstrate acceptance toward one another. Many people today grow up without a sense of identity. Those who are adopted often daydream endlessly about who their real parents were or why they were given away. Others may experience severe feelings of rejection for innumerable reasons. They grow up without a sense of "belongingness." They may have no family roots, no sense of social acceptance. The church must realize that emotional healing takes place best within the context of

caring Christians who not only bear their own burdens but share those of others. I've met people delivered from depression when five or six fellow Christians have decided that they would intercede until the emotional release came. With small support groups, those who have never felt the warmth of human affection and acceptance will begin to have a sense of identity.

Yet, there are thousands today who will not take the risk of friendship. They've been hurt so many times that they have become loners, hardened to the hurts that are destroying them. Here again, we all must reach out so that others will see that we do care, that friendships can be built and trust repaired. Every one of us needs someone who will love us regardless of what we do. And if we have no such friends, we must seek them within the confines of the Christian church.

Often, those who have experienced rejection will find other Christians and plague them with endless promises and smother them with a desire for emotional support. As a result, such people usually encounter more rejection because they unwittingly give the impression that they are an emotional drain to those who befriend them. Here again we must be sensitive to people's needs, but at the same time, we cannot let others use guilt as a motivation for our own behavior. We can support those in emotional turbulence, but there comes a time when they must also stand alone, fully responsible for their own behavior and reactions to life. Small caring communities within the church are necessary, however, for people to grow in emotional maturity.

4. *We must have a wholesome self-image.* This can only come about when we cease believing what our emotions tell us and begin believing what God says about us. We are confronted by two pictures of ourselves. One is of us as we are in Christ: sons of God; indwelt by the Holy Spirit; joined to the Son; considered as God's special possessions; and assured of future glorification. Then there

is another picture of what some of us are like in the world of our emotions: pessimistic, guilt-ridden, irritable, touchy, depressed, and worthless. Faced with such an apparent contradiction, we must make a choice. Shall we believe what God has said, or shall we follow the path of least resistance and give in to our feelings? It boils down to this: Which portrait shall we live by?

Clearly, we face a dilemma. Our emotions, inclinations, and circumstances point in one direction, whereas God's description of us points in another. We cannot live by both, for they cancel out each other. Faith means that we must not merely believe what God has said, but we must also *disbelieve* what our experiences seem to tell us.

Can our inclinations and observations actually be wrong? If I see myself as unloved, unacceptable to God, and powerless, might I be mistaken? Yes!

Left to our private observations, we would conclude that the sun revolves around the earth. What could be more obvious than that the earth is stationary and the sun moves from east to west? Yet that conclusion is dead wrong. Astronomers tell us that the sun never rises; rather, the earth turns, tilting on its axis toward the sun. Our common-sense conclusions can be misleading.

So it is with our interpretation of the events of life. Hunches and feelings are not a reliable guide to understanding the real you; God's statements invalidate our distorted self-image. If He says He loves us—and He does so repeatedly—then we *are* loved whether we feel like it or not. If we have been seated in heavenly places, we *are* in God's presence even when He seems distant. In Christ, our acceptance before God is complete and secure even when we are disappointed in ourselves.

Victory, then, is not "feeling just right." It is found by faith and faith alone. And whenever faith runs counter to feeling, we must accept faith in God's Word as the true barometer of circumstances. A few years ago, an airplane crashed into the top of a mountain. The reason?

Prior to the crash, the pilot thought that his instrument panel had gone askew. The plane's equipment indicated he was flying off course and headed for disaster. But the pilot knew better. His intuitive sense of direction told him that the instruments were wrong and his own judgment of the terrain beneath was reliable. Within an hour, he crashed.

The irony was that his judgment was *not* correct. The mechanical instruments were accurate. If he had followed their readings and rejected his own intuition, the crash would not have occurred. God wants us to fly with His equipment, the Word of God. Concentrating on who He says we are helps close the gap between our experience and our theology.

5. *We must see joy as a by-product of obedience.* Many people seek happiness and never find it because it is never found when you seek it directly. Happiness is part of the blessing that comes from doing God's will.

Perhaps a better word than happiness is *joy*. John the Baptist said that his joy was complete. He was a voice crying in the wilderness. As such, he did not draw attention to himself or speak of his gifts, but he humbly stated his calling as a servant of the Lord.

In ancient times, the friend of the bridegroom was responsible to bring the bride to the bridegroom, and after introducing them in the marriage ceremony, the friend stepped quietly away. In John 3:29, John the Baptist used this custom as an illustration of his relationship with Jesus Christ. His responsibility was to introduce people to the Bridegroom and then fade into the background. It was this that completed John's joy.

His satisfaction did not come from the large crowds that gathered to hear him preach near the Jordan River. He was not jealous of Christ's popularity, and when people left him to follow his Master, he was not grieved.

Today there is much advice on how to find lasting

happiness. Most of these suggestions stress the need to have well-defined goals such as self-fulfillment, a challenging career, or making money. At their roots, these recommendations are sinful. John the Baptist summarized what our goals should be when he said regarding Christ, "He must increase, but I must decrease" (John 3:30). John's whole life was lived to the glory of Christ.

Let's remember that the joy of the Holy Spirit does not come by seeking self-fulfillment; it comes by seeking Christ's fulfillment.

Joy (or emotional stability) is a fruit of the Holy Spirit. It comes when we accept the death of our own plans and ambitions and receive what Christ has for us. Without ending our self-rule and putting Christ completely in charge, there is no route to emotional wholeness. Someone has rightly said, "Joy is the flag flown from the castle of the heart when the King is in residence there."

If anyone should use the emotional trauma of his past as an excuse for continuing as an emotional cripple, let him ponder the nine qualities that are listed in Galatians 5:22-23 as the fruit of the Spirit. Notice that either directly or indirectly, each one touches our emotional lives: love, joy, peace, patience, kindness, goodness, faithfulness, gentleness, self-control. What a picture of emotional stability!

These are the qualities that the Holy Spirit wants to form in us as we obey God's Word. Obedience precedes blessing. Christ endured the holocaust of Gethsemane by knowing that in the end He would have emotional satisfaction (Heb. 12:2). He obeyed though He didn't feel like it; the feelings came later. No, we can't expect a life without emotional turbulence, but there can be emotional healing; the Spirit can work even amid our ups and downs. God wants us to manage our emotions; He's assured us that they need not manage us.

Application

1. What is the basis for emotional wholeness according to the Apostle Paul in Ephesians 1:3-7 and 2:4-10?

2. What is the basis for emotional disturbances according to Galatians 5:19-21?

3. What is a believer's responsibility to a person who is deeply troubled? (Acts 20:35; Rom. 15:1; Gal. 6:2; Heb. 13:3).

4. Select a passage of Scripture to memorize as a guard against Satan's attempts to lead you into emotional distress. Consider Psalm 23; Romans 8:35-39; 2 Corinthians 2:14; 1 John 3:1-2; 4:9-11; 5:4.

3

Those Feelings of Love

"LOVE conquers all!"

You've heard this expression—but is it true?

Love is the strongest positive emotion we've ever experienced. It gives us a sense of stability and self-worth. It let's us feel that we "belong" and gives life its zest.

The relationship between Christ and His church is the highest example of love. It's a love that is thoughtful, both tough and tender, and it will last forever. It's strong enough to weather our misunderstandings, hurts, and the sins which drive a wedge between us and Christ.

The love in our marriages should have the same characteristics. "Husbands, love your wives, just as Christ also loved the church and gave Himself up for her" (Eph. 5:25). If we want the details of how love reacts in the everyday circumstances of life, all of the qualities are listed in 1 Corinthians 13.

Needless to say, many marriages fall far short of this ideal. Feelings that were present at the beginning of the marriage relationship have evaporated. Often harsh words have been spoken; promises have been broken and the feelings of one of the marriage partners have been ignored. Like one man put it, "Wedlock has become a padlock that leads to a deadlock!"

Why do marriages which begin so well end so poorly? No one *intends* to have a bad marriage. Couples don't plan on ending up living under the same roof with no communication or love expressed. Yet it happens so often, that there must be some reasons for it.

Reasons for Failure
Many factors contribute to the problems found in our marriages. Let's consider several.

1. *Unrealistic expectations.* Our society stresses a romantic ideal that we all expect to find in marriage. We're given the impression that marriage leads to happiness and fulfillment without having to pay a huge price for such a relationship. Many women don't marry a man . . . they marry a dream. And when the dream fades (as it must), they are disillusioned. After that, the woman is tempted to chip away at her husband to make him into the kind of person who will make her happy. After all, she thinks her husband owes her happiness— it's his first and foremost responsibility.

The husband may make the same mistake. He expects his wife to be able to cook as well as his mother and look like Raquel Welch. She's got to measure up to his ideal or he will be tempted to find someone else who can.

Sometimes marriage is exalted to the point of idolatry: A woman may believe that her husband will change his personality and habits after marriage, as if going to the altar can effect a lasting change. Despite a stormy courtship, she actually believes that saying some words in the presence of a minister will bring fulfillment in married life. She clings to her dreams and refuses to face the fact that they will be shattered. When the bubble finally bursts, she thinks that the only way out is divorce. Walter Trobisch appropriately writes that the first lesson in love means, "One has to give up dreams, because they stand in the way of happiness" (*Love Is a Feeling to Be*

Learned, InterVarsity Press, p. 12).

2. *The myth of the greener grass.* It's easy to think that we'd be better off with a different marriage partner. After all, there are other attractive people in the world and some of them make us feel particularly special. Suddenly, we find the words *if only* in our vocabulary. "If only I had not been married so young," or "If only I had married someone else."

If happiness comes through finding the right person, then indeed we can understand why many marriage partners believe they have been shortchanged. It's inevitable that we will meet someone else who stirs our sensual drives and makes us feel important. At that point, we are tempted to opt for the greener pastures that await us in a new relationship.

It's a myth, of course. But's it's easy to believe the myth . . . and even when we *know* it's a lie, our feelings continue to behave as if our fantasies are reality.

But the emphasis in the Scriptures is not on *finding* the right person (important as that may be), but on *being* the right person. Since the fruit of the Spirit is love, we can learn to exercise this quality even if we are married to someone who is not naturally attractive. As we shall see, the best of marriages demands adjustment. And with God's help, a marriage can be rebuilt.

Regardless of the sins or wrong decisions that may have taken place in the past, no marriage can succeed unless it strikes the "if only's" from its vocabulary. Our fantasies and imaginations of what could have been actually divert us from the task at hand—namely, to see God at work in our present marriages.

3. *A failure to understand the role of conflict in marriage.* I've known married couples who become disillusioned because of disagreements that arise between them. They expect that if you marry "within the will of God," you'll agree about everything. A man from Britain upon hearing about all of the divorces on the grounds of incom-

patibility in the United States remarked accurately enough, "I thought that incompatibility was the purpose of marriage!"

You can't bring two self-centered people together into the intimate relationship of marriage without some disagreements and adjustments. Someone has appropriately observed, "At best, marriage is two imperfect people imperfectly united."

My wife and I are more happily married now than ever. We've always had a good marriage, but through years of negotiation, compromise, and communication we have had at least a few of the rough edges taken from our personalities. Our egos have sustained some bruises, but we're the better for it. It's one of the ways that God conforms us to the image of Jesus Christ.

4. *A failure to understand roles in marriage.* This isn't the place to go into detail regarding the relationship between a man and a woman in marriage except to say that the man must exercise spiritual leadership, and the woman must be submissive to his authority if the divine pattern of marriage is to be effective. I'm well aware that the marriage relationship requires balance and responsibility on both sides. But it's only when a man exercises his role as leader and provider that the woman has the security to be fulfilled within her God-given sphere in the home.

God won't let us take anything from this earth to heaven, except our children. Therefore, they must be given our highest priority and be shown the example of love and submission necessary for a sense of well-being and self-esteem. We've got to return to the Scriptures to understand where marriage partners fit in their relationships.

5. *A failure to distinguish divine and human love.* But what do we do when there are no feelings left in a marriage? Are the partners helplessly deadlocked, prisoners of a vow made in a moment of unrealistic ecstasy?

No, they are not. Every one of us can *learn* to

love . . . those feelings can be revived. We can only make progress in loving others when we realize that there is a clear distinction between human love (affection) and divine love. In Matthew 5:46-47, Jesus established what normal human love is like: "For if you love those who love you, what reward have you? Do not even the tax-gatherers do the same? And if you greet your brothers only, what do you do more than others? Do not even the Gentiles do the same?"

Jesus reminded His listeners that *human love depends on the one loved.* You greet the person in the marketplace who greets you. You are kind to your brothers because they are kind to you. You are attracted to someone because he makes you feel good. Your response is conditioned by what the other person does.

Though we don't like to admit it, all of us tend to respond to others on the basis of their appearance. Statistics prove that the cute child or the physically attractive teen gets the breaks in life. If there's a dispute in school, the teacher will normally discipline the student who is not as good looking. Hollywood has strengthened that basic human reaction so that we unconsciously accept people on the basis of their appearance. Add the powerful stimulus of sexual attractiveness and you've got a strong force with which to contend. And if the person has an attractive personality, that is a powerful package. No wonder it's easy to "fall in love" with such a person.

The Bible beautifully describes human love in a poem by Solomon: "How beautiful you are, my darling, how beautiful you are! Your eyes are like doves behind your veil; your hair is like a flock of goats that have descended from Mount Gilead. Your lips are like a scarlet thread, and your mouth is lovely. Your temples are like a slice of pomegranate behind your veil" (Song 4:1, 3). Is it any wonder that people say love is blind?

Now notice what else Solomon said: "You are all together beautiful, my darling, and there is no blemish in you. You have made my heart beat faster, my sister, my bride; you have made my heart beat faster with a single glance of your eyes, with a single strand of your necklace. How beautiful is your love, my sister, my bride! How much better is your love than wine, and the fragrance of your oils than all kinds of spices!" (4:7, 9-10) That man was in love!

Human love is God-ordained and God-given; it makes life exciting. We all need acceptance and a sense of well-being to be emotionally well-balanced. Yet human love has its limitations.

In the first place, *human love is subject to change*. Why? Because it depends on the one being loved; it needs to be fed by the stimulus that the one who is loved provides. If that changes, love may change.

After I spoke in a large church in the Midwest, a lady came to speak to me. She was physically attractive, but had a cast on her arm and part of her face was scarred. Her four-year-old daughter was at her side. The woman told me about a fire in their house two years earlier in which she had been severely burned. She was in the hospital for several weeks and underwent extensive treatment. Even now, she was in a partial body cast. But when her husband saw how bad her scars were and realized that they would never disappear, he left her. He "fell in love" and married a younger girl, leaving his former wife and daughter behind.

So does love conquer all? Don't believe it! Human love has clear limits because it is based on something in you or about you—it's to my advantage to be associated with you. But when you are no longer of use to me, my human love fades.

A second limitation to human love is its *transferability*. It can be transferred to someone else and you can "fall in love" with someone who isn't your marriage partner. John may have married Jan, but when he meets Kathy, he finds her to be more to his liking. She listens to him, accepts his moods, and at last he feels that he has met someone who understands him perfectly!

God wants us to realize that marriage cannot be based on human attractiveness alone. The Bible doesn't give specific guidance on whom we are to marry, except that they should have the desirable qualities of Christian character. We can depend on God to give us divine love which is strong enough to survive the rough spots in life.

My wife is a very attractive person. She is easy to love on a human level. Yet even in our marriage, we have discovered that there are times when human love is not enough. That's why the Bible tells us about divine love—so that we can go on loving even during the difficult times.

What Is Divine Love?
Divine love is based on and dependent on the lover. It is not a feeling, for with it we can even love our enemies!

A couple who went to a marriage counselor expected him to recommend divorce because there was no feeling left in their relationship. When he told the husband that he was to love his wife like Christ loved the church, the husband replied, "That's impossible!" Then the counselor said, "But the Bible says you are to love your neighbor—can't you love her with that kind of love?" Even then the man felt that it was beyond him and said such love was impossible. So the counselor replied, "Then you have to begin at a different level. . . . You've got to love your wife, for the Bible says we must love our enemies!"

In contrast to human love, divine love always involves *sacrificial action.* "But God demonstrates His own love toward us, in that while we were yet sinners, Christ died for us" (Rom. 5:8). Long before we could respond to God, He was already responding to us.

Divine love then is more than sentiment or even sympathy. It's easy to say that we love the world, but actually we can only love people for whom we are able to sacrifice. It's easy to say that we love others, but it's proven by our actions toward a son-in-law or an aged parent.

Christ specified those actions that accompany divine love. First He says, "Bless those who curse you" (Luke 6:28). Negatively, it means that you do not speak evil of your enemies, that there is no indiscriminate discussion of their failures. Positively, it means that you actually learn to say good things about your enemies.

Sometimes in marriage counseling, I've asked the husband to write down five good characteristics about his wife and vice versa. Usually the couple finds it hard to think of a single commendable quality, but once they get started they are surprised. It's such characteristics we ought to have in our minds whenever our enemies come up in conversations so that we can *bless* them rather than curse them.

A second action Christ suggested was, "Do good to those who hate you" (v. 27). Paul exhorted us to feed an enemy if he is hungry and give him a drink if he is thirsty (Rom. 12:20). We should take such positive action whether we feel like it or not. Our goal is to become imitators of God. "For He causes His sun to rise on the evil and the good, and sends rain on the righteous and the unrighteous" (Matt. 5:45). God blesses without discrimination and so should we.

The third command of Jesus is, "Pray for those who mistreat you" (Luke 6:28). On the cross Christ gave us a beautiful example when He prayed, "Father, forgive them; for they do not know what they are doing" (Luke 23:34). Remember Stephen's prayer while the stones were striking him, "Lord, do not hold this sin against them!" (Acts 7:60)

We ought to pray that those who have wronged us

will be forgiven by God. We ought to pray earnestly that they will experience the richness of the Father's love and forgiveness. Then we also ought to pray that God will bless them and make their lives a blessing. That's divine love in action.

There's a fourth command I would like to add on the basis of other passages in the New Testament, and that is that we ought to depend on the Holy Spirit. There is a supernatural giving that the Holy Spirit is able to work within us. We discover that we cannot love in a given situation, but when we depend on the Holy Spirit, He gives us the motivation to actually take the initiative. When we finally initiate action, we discover that we really do begin to love again, to love our enemies.

That is how you really gain control over your feelings. When you obey the Word of God, He takes those actions of love and rebuilds the human affections drained away through the pressures of life. Even though human love may have disappeared, God can rebuild those feelings of affection as we start acting as Jesus commanded.

You say, "You don't really know what you are talking about. You have never been abused the way I have." Maybe I haven't, but I am only too well aware of how people treat each other. I can readily understand why in many relationships there are no feelings left, why the very things that were once attractive now cause you to feel revulsion toward a person. Human love simply is not strong enough to weather all the storms of life. But when we exercise divine love, which is not a feeling based on sentiment or on whether you fulfill me or not, but an action taken as a result of my commitment to you, then God can mend the relationship. You will experience the tremendous power of God's love as you actually do what Jesus commanded.

A woman who had been sexually abused by her stepfather from the age of 17 on into her early 20s married a fine man. She discovered that she could not love her husband, because as soon as he showed her any affection, it would elicit all those ugly feelings of hatred she had toward her stepfather. She went to her pastor for counseling as a last resort.

"Your first step is to forgive your stepfather. If you do not forgive him, there is no hope of you ever loving your husband," the pastor told her very kindly. He knew she represented many people who cannot really love because they have never forgiven someone who abused them. He asked her to turn to the passage of Scripture that gives us the action plan for loving our enemies, and he worked out a homework assignment. She was so desperate that she decided to go ahead with the assignment.

I guess she did a little research, because she did come up with some good things to say about her stepfather. She discovered, much to her surprise, that he had some good qualities. She actually practiced saying some of those good things. Whenever a conversation would start about her past life or regarding him, she would be sure to say something good. She refused to make any insinuations or negative remarks. You will remember that God says He judges us by the words that come out of our mouths, for if we speak evil it only increases the evil. If we speak good, God is responsible for multiplying the good.

She also remembered that her stepfather had a birthday coming up. So she baked a cake for his birthday. And because the Bible says to pray for our enemies, she determined to pray for him three times a day. She said, "I am going to pray that God will forgive his sin and that he will be brought to repentance. I am going to pray that God will bless him. I am going to pray that God is going to use that man and change him for God's glory." And she did it.

How did she feel about doing all this? In reality, every fiber of her body revolted against the idea. She would have been a hypocrite if she had said at that time, "I really love this man." But obedience to God's Word is never hypocrisy. So despite how she felt, she went about her assignment, week in and week out. Several weeks later, she saw her stepfather in a supermarket. She noticed he was buying some groceries and then watched him walk to his car. Suddenly she discovered that her feelings had changed. Instead of all those ugly feelings of hurt and bitterness that always surfaced when she saw him, she realized that she actually had some human affection for him. She later told her pastor, "If it were not for our past relationship, I would have gone and put my arm around him." Then she added, "Furthermore, I now love my husband." She had experienced that human feelings can be managed when they are overwhelmed by divine love.

Human love is a response to good things happening to us. Divine love is triggered by an act of the will. That's why an act of commitment to love as God has loved us gets our feelings under divine management.

Can you actually learn to love your disagreeable mate? The answer is yes. You must choose to say no to yourself—your cherished dreams and fantasies. You can no longer think of whom you ought to have married and what that other mate could have done for you. No longer can you daydream about how someone else would have made you *feel*.

Such feelings of self-pity must be confessed for what they are: sin. Then you must begin a positive course of action, with dependence upon the Holy Spirit. Meditate in the Scriptures (memorizing 1 Corinthians 13 would be a good beginning), because the root of the problem is spiritual. *Your relationship with your mate will be determined by your relationship with God.* God will use this experience in your life to strengthen your relationship with Him. Remember, divine love involves a choice, dependence, and faith. We can learn to love *anyone*.

Application

1. The best exposition of divine love is 1 Corinthians 13. Here Paul listed 15 qualities of love. Write down each one with a practical example to illustrate it.

2. "The reason people can't get along is sin—take sin away and the bickering is over." Do you agree or disagree? Give examples of the kinds of sins that create conflicts within the home. What kinds of conflicts may not be the result of sin?

3. Meditate on 1 John 4:18-19. Why can't fear and love coexist?

4. Love being a gift of the Holy Spirit, how does Paul teach that we can receive the Spirit's power? (Gal. 5:18-26)

5. What should a married person do who is falling in love with another partner? Specifically, what steps should be taken to prevent physical and emotional involvement? Answers to keeping oneself from sexual sin can be found in Proverbs 5.

4

Defeating Depression

BEAUTIFUL. Intelligent. Well-groomed. Those adjectives describe the woman who came to see me after a meeting. Though she was quite wealthy and even had a reasonably happy marriage, she was contemplating suicide. She, along with millions of others, was suffering from America's number one emotional disorder: Depression.

Perhaps depression is the darkest of all negative emotions. Someone has called it "a dark tunnel with not a ray of light." Another refers to it as the time when "your emotions weigh a ton and you want to die." Another man describes it this way: "It was horror and hell. I was at the bottom of the deepest pit there ever was. I was worthless and unforgivable. I was as good as—no, worse than—dead."

No one seems to be immune to depression. Consider the following statements: "I am the subject of depression of spirit so fearful that I hope none of you ever gets to such extremes of wretchedness as I go to. . . . Personally, I have often passed through this dark valley [of depression]." And here's another quote, "For more than a week I was close to the gates of death and

43

hell. I trembled in all my members. Christ was wholly
lost. I was shaken by desperation and blasphemy of
God."

Who spoke these words? Carnal Christians who were
living with one foot in the world? A new convert who
didn't understand the basis of God's acceptance? Hardly.
The first statement was made by one of the world's
greatest and most successful preachers, Charles Haddon
Spurgeon. The second was from the great reformer, Martin Luther.

Generally speaking, there are three primary causes of
depression.

Physical—Chemical Causes

Physical illnesses can trigger depression. Diabetes, a mal-
functioning thyroid gland, and other ailments can cause
us to be preoccupied with our "blue" moods. Even physical exhaustion can lead to that "burned out" feeling that
may bring about pessimism and despair.

There also is a link between the chemistry of the body
and depression. It's obvious that drugs or alcohol can
cause psychological "lows" and even the despair that
leads to suicide.

Whether the body left to itself can become chemically
depleted and hence cause depression is disputed. Some
researchers are unconvinced that depression can be
traced to a chemical imbalance in the brain. However, it
is known that medication can relieve depression to some
extent. This enables the patient to feel better and cope
with life. Counseling can then be more valuable because
the patient can *do* the kinds of activities that will relieve
his emotional turbulence. Medication is not a permanent
solution to depression—except in those rare cases where
a patient is not willing to function or respond to counsel.

Unfortunately, some psychiatrists wish to reduce all
depression to physical—chemical factors. On an airplane
I read a magazine article entitled "New Ways of Coping

with Guilt." It was a discussion of new drugs designed to deaden emotional pain. In other words, the writer assumed that no problem was spiritual, but purely physical and chemical.

But actually, depression is almost always psychological (our reaction to circumstances) or spiritual (the result of sin which we refuse to face). As we shall see, depression is often a disease of the soul caused by moral failure. The cure is repentance and restoration. Someone has well said, "Counselors are trying to make many people comfortable whom God is trying to make miserable!"

Psychological Depression

This kind of depression comes about because of upsetting circumstances. The sudden death of a loved one, the news that we've got a tumor, or the "letdown" experienced after the birth of a baby—all of these events, along with a host of others, can lead us into depression.

The Bible contains many specific examples of this kind of depression. When David learned that his son Absalom had been killed, he was crushed so deeply that he lost his perspective on what had happened. Of course, as a father he was grieved because of Absalom's violent death. But after all, Absalom was a rebel and wanted to kill his own father. The people who had rescued David risked their lives in fighting against Absalom's forces. David's grief was normal, but because he ignored the feelings of his friends, he allowed his grief to cloud his perspective.

What is more, David was emotionally paralyzed; he could not function as a king. Joab had to go to him directly and point out that his grief was excessive; David simply had to pull himself together and start running the kingdom (2 Sam. 19:1-7).

Or consider Job. He was in such despair that he longed for death. He questioned why he was ever born, he was angry because he saw the light of day. Notice these symptoms. There was extreme sadness, "Where-fore is light given to him that is in misery, and life unto the bitter in soul" (Job 3:20,KJV). Also, he desired to die, "Who long for death, but there is none, and dig for it more than for hidden treasures" (v. 21). Furthermore, Job couldn't sleep, "When I lie down I say, 'When shall I arise?' But the night continues and I am continually toss-ing until dawn" (7:4).

Job was reacting to tragedy. He had lost his children, his health, and his possessions. His wife encouraged him to curse God and die (2:9). Surely none of us would react differently to such news. Destruction outside of us leads to despair within us.

Even Jesus Christ, who was sinless, experienced a form of depression in Gethsemane when He contemplat-ed the horror of becoming identified with the sins of the whole world. This should rid us of the notion that all depression is the result of sin. Sometimes, it is simply our response to the fluctuating circumstances of life.

It's important to understand the difference between psychological depression (which we all experience) and the kind of depression which engulfs us when we handle these experiences incorrectly. Prolonged depression comes when we allow our feelings to control us. Conse-quently, guilt is added to the disappointments we al-ready have; soon we become negative, feel worthless, and we actually hate ourselves. Depression increases and there seems to be no way out. Thus, some people contin-ue in a state of melancholy long after the tragedies have passed.

Such depression is a sign of spiritual failure. Some-times we may be angry with God or filled with self-pity. We may not be willing to face these attitudes, but God is getting our attention; He is goading us into facing sins we have rationalized. As David found during those long nights when he lived with unconfessed sin, "Day and night Your hand was heavy upon me" (Ps. 32:4, NIV).

The Bible gives numerous examples of depression caused by spiritual failure. Sins that we nurture rather than confess and forsake, and attitudes which are negative rather than positive can all lead to emotional pain. Let's consider some examples.

Spiritual Depression

In Deuteronomy 28:65 the Lord spoke of the consequences that would come to the Israelites if they disobeyed Him. Among the tragedies listed, one is "despair of soul." There is firm evidence that much depression is due to *disobedience;* in a word, it is caused by sin.

And what particular sins might lead to depression? Jealousy led Saul to become manic-depressive. The women of Israel sang, "Saul has slain his thousands, and David his ten thousands" (1 Sam. 18:7). The result is that "Saul looked at David with suspicion from that day on" (v. 9). The next day, an evil spirit from God came mightily upon Saul and he tried to kill David with his spear (vv. 10-11).

Notice the characteristics of a man consumed with jealousy. First, he is suspicious. David had not made any moves to snatch the kingdom from Saul; indeed, he refused to lift a hand against Saul to capture it. But the king *suspected* that David would do so.

I've known husbands who were violently suspicious of their wives. They would call home several times a day just to make sure that their wives were not visiting at a friend's house. Almost always these suspicions can be traced to premarital sex—either between the husband and wife or other promiscuous relationships. These sins, if not fully faced and forsaken, rear their ugly heads to torment the marriage relationship. Such jealousy produces depression; the depression in turn magnifies the jealousy.

A second characteristic of a jealous man is his vindictiveness. Saul lashed out at David with revenge, trying to pin him against the wall with a spear. There was really nothing to be angry about—David had done no harm. But the suspicious king could not cope with his hostility except by trying to "even the score" when there was really no evil in David's heart.

Irrational? Yes. But so are the responses of any person who is eaten daily by envy and mistrust. He's being destroyed by a sin he doesn't want to face.

Are you surprised by the statement that "an evil spirit from God came mightily upon Saul, and he raved in the midst of the house"? (v. 10) God allowed a demon to torment Saul. That sometimes happens when we nurse cherished grudges that we refuse to surrender to God. Our punishment is increased; our guilt is magnified. Jealousy can be the cause of deep depression.

Unresolved *anger* can also cause depression. Look at the example of Jonah. He was surely one of the strangest prophets God ever called to the ministry. He was an immensely successful evangelist—the whole city of Nineveh repented because of his preaching. Was Jonah pleased? No. He was angry, violently angry.

Jonah hated the people of Nineveh. They had often warred against Israel and were used by God to punish the nation. Furthermore, they were non-Jewish; they were not among the "chosen of God." When God lifted the threat of His judgment because of their repentance, Jonah was sorely displeased (Jonah 3:5, 10; 4:1).

He was angry for another reason. Jonah hated the weather in Nineveh. It was hot, *very* hot, with a scorching east wind. One evening God graciously appointed a plant to grow up over Jonah to shield him from the burning heat. That made him feel better; indeed, he seemed to be on the way to emotional recovery.

Then wham! A worm came to eat the plant and the sun beat down on Jonah's head once again. What is more, the hot east wind began to blow with more fury than ever. Jonah became faint and longed for death (4:6-

8). Notice his impertinent attitude, "Then God said to Jonah, 'Do you have good reason to be angry about the plant?' And he said, 'I have good reason to be angry, even to death'" (v. 9).

Jonah was angry with God and that led to self-pity. He believed he was being subjected to cruel and unusual punishment. People whom he hated were being blessed by God and a plant which kept him cool had been cut down. What did he do to deserve this? He could only think of one way out of his dilemma: *Death.*

People who are angry often experience depression. They long for death because they believe it is the only exit that they have open to them. In their hearts, they think that their anger is directed toward people. But like Jonah, their anger is *ultimately* directed against God. Their self-pity controls them and despair rules their hearts.

Recently, I received a phone call from a girl who wanted help to escape from the cycle of suicidal depression. A few questions immediately brought deep resentment to the surface. She was angry with her father who had left the family to live with a teenage girl. She was bitter against her friends and resentful of her mother and brother; her bitterness was deep and vindictive.

Expressions of self-pity often surface among those who are resentful. Many hours are spent rehearsing in great detail all of the wrongs done against them. Often such a depressed person prays but receives no relief, because even the prayertime is used to recount all the wrongs done against him or her. Every insult, whether real or imagined, is meticulously added to the list of reasons why they have "a right" to be bitter.

Obviously, we must be sensitive to such people. With the breakup of families and the alarming rise of child abuse, many people have indeed been treated unfairly. Our world is filled with injustice. We can readily understand why resentment and self-pity develop. But though we must show compassion, we cannot agree that such people have a right to feel the way they do. For unless they give up that right, their depression will never leave.

People resent being told that they are guilty of self-pity. All of us resist the idea that we must give up feeling sorry for ourselves. Yet if we insist on our right to continue with our present feelings, we are closing the door to freedom.

Third, *guilt* may lead to depression. Let's not underestimate the effect of guilt in our lives. For example, I've heard people who are living in sexual immorality say, "We've learned to work through our guilt." What they really mean is that they have learned to ignore their guilt or to talk themselves out of it. Yet the consequences of sin are built into the nature of life. We cannot violate God's commandments without choking our relationship with Him.

Can guilt cause a depression severe enough to lead to suicide? Consider Judas, the man who betrayed Christ. When he saw that Christ had been condemned, he felt remorse and returned the 30 pieces of silver to the chief priests. Of course they were not sympathetic to his half-hearted confession, "I have sinned by betraying innocent blood" (v. 4). So he threw the silver into the sanctuary and departed and then went and hanged himself (Matt. 27:3-5).

What led to the guilt-ridden remorse that Judas experienced? It was *greed*—his insatiable desire for money. He was the treasurer for the disciples and apparently had been pilfering all along. Yet he did not receive enough money to satisfy himself. He needed more.

Judas loved money, silver in particular. He thought that with 30 extra pieces he would get ahead financially before he betrayed Christ. His focus was on the money; doubtless he visualized all that he would be able to purchase with it. But after he had the money in his hand, he began to think of his sin; the money meant nothing. The satisfaction of having the silver was overshadowed by the weight of his guilt. No doubt if Judas had lived in our time, he could have talked to his psychiatrist and received some drugs to deaden the pain of his deep remorse. But since such help was not available to him, he did what 25,000 Americans do every year. He committed suicide.

It's important to notice that Judas' remorse was exploited by Satan. You'll recall that after the Lord had assembled the disciples for the Last Supper, Satan personally entered into Judas to enable him to betray Christ (John 13:27). We have no reason to think that Judas asked for Satan's help. It's just that this man had given territory in his life to satanic impulses, and Satan welcomed himself into Judas' life. Remember that Satan and his demons need no formal invitation. All they seek is an unbeliever hostile to the truth or a Christian who lives in persistent sin, and they will take as much territory as they can get.

Again, the root cause is sin. To confess our sins means that we agree fully with God; we take His perspective. But when we refuse to agree with Him and rationalize our behavior, we may soon be experiencing a nagging emotional pain. While others around us seem to be happy, we wonder whether we will ever smile again. *Everything* will appear futile.

So What Should We Do?
Here are some steps that will help us pinpoint the problem and get on with a solution.

1. *If possible, identify the cause.* Sometimes that's difficult, and in a few instances it may be impossible. Depression sometimes hits us "out of the blue" without any known cause. In these instances, it would be wise to consult a family doctor or a counselor to see if the cause can be found.

Often the cause is more readily apparent. It may be

because of those painful experiences of life or physical weariness. Or it might be due to sin—guilt, jealousy, anger, or fear. In fact, depression may come because of sins that we think have already been taken care of.

I know of a woman who experienced depression for nearly 20 years without any relief. But finally one day in a moment of honesty, she confided to her pastor that she had had an illegitimate child whom she killed with her own hands. Though she was a Christian, the past haunted her and she had to experience the freedom of God's forgiveness. When her pastor helped her do that, the depression left.

Remember, depression sometimes can come because of false guilt as well. A woman who was constantly told by her father, "God is going to punish you for your disobedience," later interpreted every tragedy as a fulfillment of her father's words. The slightest difficulty upset her, for she thought that she was under God's condemnation. Only when she saw God in a new light, was she able to accept the routine of daily living without depression.

If there has been incest in the family, a child often experiences depression in later life. Here again, it may be because of false guilt—for the child is not responsible for the parent's behavior. Yet because the child's virginity has been taken away, the unresolved feelings of guilt may lead to hostility and depression.

God is able to rid us of both kinds of guilt. The real guilt is forgiven through Christ. The false guilt is also cleansed from the conscience so that we can live without self-incrimination. If necessary, we must forgive ourselves after God has forgiven us, or simply rest in the assurance that we are *fully accepted* in Christ. God wants to rid us of all guilt. Our pasts should not control our futures.

2. *Refuse to pull down the shades of self-pity.* Depression causes us to withdraw; there's a tendency to be alone.

Martin Luther was right when he said, "Isolation is poison for the depressed person, for through this the devil attempts to keep him in his power."

We must steadfastly resist this temptation. Even when we don't feel like it, we should seek out people and situations which generate joy.

3. *Fulfill your God-given responsibilities.* Depressed people often want to stay in bed, lounging around, waiting for their gloom to dissipate. Often they neglect their families or jobs. This actually increases the guilt, and with it their depression becomes more severe. When we *must* function and stop pampering ourselves, our depression recedes. God honors obedience.

4. *Develop a life of praise.* Saul's fits of depression were at least temporarily relieved when David played his harp. The probable reason is that the evil spirit (sent by God to torment Saul) withdrew when confronted by music that exalted the praises of Jehovah (1 Sam. 16:23).

Satan hates praise to God; indeed he is defeated when we learn to give thanks in everything since it is an affront to his control. We should memorize psalms of praise so that we can honor God in thanksgiving and worship.

What if your depression continues? God may be teaching you to walk by faith, not by sight. Remember that your emotional trauma does not separate you from Christ's love. God is still with you.

A woman who experienced two full years of depression asked, "Why didn't somebody tell me it would get better someday?" Then she added, "I would have been able to cope more easily."

God may be turning your night into day!

Application

1. What factors may have caused a man of God like Elijah to experience such depression that he longed to die? (1 Kings 19:4)

2. God promised Israel fear and despondency if they would not obey Him (Deut. 28:65). What sins have we committed as a nation that may be contributing to the emotional malaise of this generation?

3. What did Christ do to enable Him to survive the emotional depression of Gethsemane? (Matt. 26:36-42) Take particular note of His honesty and the role His friends were asked to have during those difficult hours.

4. In Psalm 77, Asaph expresses the deepest anguish of depression. But in the last half of the psalm, his spirit improves immeasurably. What made the difference?

5. In overcoming guilt, we must remember that we need not confess the same specific sin twice (unless, of course, we commit it again). Rather, we must learn to praise the Lord for His forgiveness. Find all the verses you can that assure us that our sins are forgiven and blotted out.

6. Study Job 1:1-3 and 13-19 to find out what caused Job's self-pity in Job 3. How was Job's attitude eventually changed? (chap. 42)

5

Living with Rejection

DORIE had never known the love of a mother. Day after day she looked after her younger sister, hoping that her mother would show her the same affection her younger sister received. Yet even though her mother would cuddle her sister, tuck her into bed, and kiss her good-night, she brushed off all of Dorie's attempts to win that same love.

One day, both Dorie and her sister were taken to an orphanage. Their mother visited them only twice in seven years. Eventually Dorie and her sister were placed in a foster home, where they were beaten and fed leftovers. From this couple, Dorie discovered that her mother was a waitress. One day, she and her sister set out to find their mother, going from cafe to cafe. At the end of the day they found her, only to be rudely rejected.

By the time she was 18, Dorie had been in many foster homes and had been so badly beaten that her back was sometimes a mass of welts and cuts. She had never heard anyone say, "I love you."

Dorie's example of rejection is not an isolated case, for as she travels and speaks to women's groups today, she

is besieged by women and girls with similar experiences
of deep rejection. One reason is the escalating divorce
rate. Statistics show that one-half of all children born in
the United States will at one point live with only one
parent. Many not only feel that they have been rejected
by one parent, but they also feel responsible for what
has happened in their families. Often they have to sit
through ugly and grueling court battles, seeing one parent reject the other—and them.

Unwanted children are often victims of rejection. They
may have been conceived out of wedlock (as Dorie had
been, she discovered later), or their parents really did
not want children at all. From early childhood, these
children sense that they are not wanted. They are
pushed aside as an inconvenience, a nuisance. Their
most desperate attempts to gain attention only arouse
anger and resentment in their parents. As the days drag
by, these children sink deeper into rejection. Many become runaways, and often become victims of those pan-
dering to the sexual appetites of unscrupulous men and
women.

Even in homes where children are accepted and loved,
one or more may experience tacit rejection. The oldest
child may be the most brilliant, and the parents begin to
favor that child, making unfavorable comparisons that
deeply wound the second child. Other parents favor the
prettiest daughter, giving her special attention and privi-
leges. The implicit rejection of the less intelligent, the
less beautiful, causes deep feelings of rejection. These
children may then feel a need to make all kinds of special
efforts to gain favorable attention. If these efforts fail,
such children may resort to negative behavior as a last
attempt to be seen and heard.

Rejection may come in adult life—and be just as traumatic. Ann had been married for 20 years and had spent
her life raising the 8 children the Lord had given her and
her husband. Deeply religious, she saw that they all

went to Sunday School regularly with her. Her husband was king in her life; he could do no wrong. Though she had been aware of some cooling in his ardor, she was unprepared when he told her he was getting a divorce and marrying his secretary. Devastated by this rejection, she eventually was admitted to a mental hospital. Two years after this rejection, she set out to take her own life.

Or consider Jim, who had been a highly successful businessman until his mid-40s. As vice-president in charge of marketing, he exuded self-confidence. Then his company merged with a much larger one. In the merger, he was forced out. Two years later he was still floundering, convinced he was doomed to be a failure. Repeated rejections in his attempts to find a new position robbed him of his self-confidence. The fact that his wife had to work to keep bread on the table only increased his feelings of guilt, rejection, and anger.

The Results of Rejection

This feeling of rejection is the seedbed for a whole cluster of negative emotions. Rejected people usually feel terribly alone. Their loneliness can lead to depression, despair, and attempts at suicide. Or the person becomes indifferent and uncaring to those who have rejected him, saying in effect, "I don't care what you think. I am going to be indifferent toward you because you have wronged me." Children may simply disappear and never notify their parents where they have gone. Brothers and sisters refuse to show at family occasions where the other is present. Such bitterness may transfer to those on the job, so that the rejected person refuses to talk to fellow employees.

Frequently, rejection leads to demonic activity. I don't know of another emotion that is so often exploited by demonic powers. Overwhelmed by their rejections, people cannot seem to break out of their shells. They feel worthless, totally insecure, full of despair and hopelessness. Somehow, these feelings so color their thinking that they see no way out of their prison. Satan has them bound.

We read in Proverbs, "The spirit of a man can endure his sickness, but a broken spirit who can bear?" (Prov. 18:14) You and I can put up with bodily injury; you can break your leg and recover; you can experience many physical pains. Yet what happens when the spirit within you is wounded? The writer of Proverbs leaves it simply as a question, as though the answer is obvious. The emotionally wounded person cannot deal with feelings of rejection on the basis of the intellect alone. You can say, "I will reject them. I will refuse them. I will not think about them." But those emotional feelings stay in your subconscious and will surface constantly unless you deal with them at a deep level of consciousness.

Christ's Rejection

If denying those feelings is not the way to deal with rejection, what is? I believe the answer is found in Isaiah 53. Based on the insights contained in this pasasge, I believe it is possible for you, no matter what your background, to move from rejection to acceptance. You can move from self-pity to praise, from bitter feelings to feelings of love. God has made provision to heal those feelings of rejection.

Before you read any more, get your Bible and thoughtfully read Isaiah 53. Underline the words that express rejection and the resulting feelings. Then underline what Jesus, who is the focus of Isaiah 53, has done for you despite the rejection He experienced. When you have done this, keep your Bible open beside you as you read the rest of this chapter.

First, I want you to notice that *Jesus Christ's rejection was complete.* In verse 2, Jesus is compared to a plant, a tender shoot that grows up out of parched ground. That is in contrast to someone who was brought up, as it were, in a well-watered garden. Jesus Christ, the Son of God, grew up in a society that rejected Him, in "parched ground."

Consider the lineage of Jesus. You'll find prostitutes and other notable sinners listed. Christ could hardly boast of His family tree! Beyond that, Jesus Christ was raised in the town of Nazareth so that He might be called a Nazarene (Matt. 2:23). The city of Nazareth was a despised city to the high society of that day. It was the ghetto of Israel, the wrong side of the tracks. That is why in the Gospels, people referred with derision to Jesus as a Nazarene. He had the stigma of Nazareth, and that was one reason why He was rejected by society.

Jesus was also rejected by His peers. Notice that in Isaiah 53:3 He is described as "rejected of men" (KJV), or as we read in the *New American Standard Bible*, "He was despised and forsaken of men." He was a "man of sorrows, and acquainted with grief." Jesus Christ was ridiculed and mocked; the people tried to push Him over the brow of a hill at one time. When it finally came time for Him to die, the Herodians and Sadducees, who could never agree on anything, decided to overlook their differences so they could unite against Jesus Christ.

How did Jesus bear that rejection? Did He take it stoically? The Bible clearly tells us that the answer is no. Already in the Old Testament prophecy in Isaiah 53, He was described as "a man of sorrows, and acquainted with grief."

Are you acquainted with grief? Do you rise in the morning with grief? Do you go to bed at night with grief? Jesus Christ was well-acquainted with grief. "He came to His own, and those who were His own did not receive Him" (John 1:11). His own people rejected Him, and because of that Jesus Christ received great heaviness of spirit. Even His friend Judas rejected Him and betrayed Him. So Jesus experienced the upheaval of emotions that you experience when you are rejected. In fact, we read that Jesus was of such heaviness of spirit that He was "like one from whom men hide their face" (Isa. 53:3). He was like a leper.

Have you ever seen someone who sorrows so much, and is under such heaviness of spirit, that you don't even want to look at him? That's the way Jesus was.

It is true that in the midst of this there was joy in doing the Father's will. Jesus did have this satisfaction in the middle of that rejection and hurt. It is important, however, to see clearly that Jesus Christ experienced the rejection of society and His peers. He knows what it is like to be abandoned.

By now you may be saying, "Yes, I agree that all this is true, but I have an even worse story to tell. Jesus Christ was accepted by His parents, Mary and Joseph, but I was rejected by my parents. Jesus Christ was never married, so He does not know what it is like to be rejected by a lover, a wife, or a husband."

Let me discuss a third form of rejection experienced by Jesus, a rejection more excruciating and difficult than any rejection experienced by you. Not only was He rejected by society, by His peers—but *He was also rejected by God, His Father.* Look at Isaiah 53:4: "Surely our griefs He Himself bore, and our sorrows He carried; yet we ourselves esteemed Him stricken, smitten of God, and afflicted." And in verse 10 we read, "But the Lord was pleased to crush Him." When Jesus died on the cross, He cried out, "My God, My God, why hast Thou forsaken Me?" (Matt. 27:46) It was as if He were saying, "I can understand why men would forsake Me, but, O, My God, why hast *Thou* forsaken Me?" He was abandoned by His Father.

You must remember that Jesus Christ was and is God. As such, He was making a payment for the sins of the world. That payment was to God. God was dying for God. That is a tremendous mystery. Yet Jesus Christ knew in those moments on the cross what it was like to have the Father, with whom He had such fellowship, turn His back on Him. At that point, Jesus became legally guilty of every sin that was or ever will be committed. He became *legally* guilty of incest, genocide, adultery, lying, and stealing. Because of that, He died alone. Abandoned. It was the worst form of rejection a person could ever experience.

Many of you may be feeling rejected because of some physical defect, real or imagined. You were not as beautiful, not as bright, not as obedient, not as talented as someone else. You can take heart: Jesus Christ, the sinless One, experienced deep rejection too. That proves that your rejection is unrelated to your intrinsic worth as an individual. You are worth just as much as someone who grew up in a home where he or she was accepted. Get your pen and underline that sentence. *In the sight of God, in terms of your real value as a person, you are just as important and just as worthy of acceptance as any other person you know.*

Our Acceptance

Here is good news! *Christ's rejection secured our acceptance.* That prophetic passage in Isaiah 53 teaches us that Jesus Christ bore two things for us—at least two things. One is our sin. In verse 5 we read, "But He was pierced through for our transgressions, He was crushed for our iniquities; the chastening for our well-being fell upon Him, and by His scourging we are healed." That is possible because "the Lord has caused the iniquity of us all to fall on Him" (v. 6). The sinless Jesus, the truly perfect God-Man, died in our place. Theologians refer to it as the substitutionary death of Jesus.

During the U.S. Civil War, a man who had lost his wife and had several children to care for was drafted. He did not want to go, so a young man in the community volunteered to go in his place. He was killed in the war. But as a result, the man with a family did not have to go to war. There was no way the government could force him to go into battle, because he had already gone in the person of the young man. Someone had taken his place. In the same way, Jesus Christ was hanged on the cross in our place. He bore our sins and transgressions, accepting the punishment due us for our sins.

Yet Jesus also bore something else, our negative emotions. Isaiah 53:4 clearly states, "Surely our griefs He Himself bore, and our sorrows He carried." Christ not only died that you could be forgiven and free from sin, but He also bore your sorrow, your rejection, and your hurt. Consequently, all of those ugly emotions that rise up within you to make you miserable may be carried away. As a result you can say, "Thank God, I am free."

Just imagine someone sitting down beside you as you are struggling with rejection and saying, "You know, I think you have carried those emotions too long. Why don't you give them to me. I'll carry them for you for a week. Maybe I'll give them back to you then, but I'll just take them home for a while." Wouldn't it be nice if after the week the person did not want to give them back to you? He would simply say, "I'll bear them for you." You could be free!

Jesus Christ did just that for you. He was hanged on the cross. He experienced all those rejections and sorrows, those hurts and the abandonment by God, so that you would not have to endure them anymore. Yes, Jesus Christ took upon Himself our sins *and* our sorrows and ugly feelings.

That does not mean that we will never sorrow, that we will never have any bad emotions. Sometime we *do* have them. An analogy is the biblical truth that Jesus Christ tasted death for every man. That doesn't mean that we die to our humanity. But it does mean that our sorrow can be turned into joy as we understand that He becomes our burden-bearer because He died in our place.

It is important that we recognize the significance of

Jesus Christ's substitutionary death. Examine Isaiah 53:11: "As a result of the anguish of His soul, He will see it and be satisfied; by His knowledge the righteous One, My Servant, will justify the many, as He will bear their iniquities." Inasmuch as all our sins were placed upon Jesus Christ, and He died for our sins, all of Jesus Christ's righteousness is now imputed to us. We really have made an exchange, and we certainly got a good deal! Jesus Christ says, "I will receive all your sins." In return, He transfers to us His righteousness.

This is why the Bible says that believers are highly favored of the Lord. It is not a case of God's beginning to tolerate you, saying in effect, "Now I can put up with you." No! The Bible clearly teaches that you are highly favored of the Lord, accepted in the Beloved. All the wonderful thoughts God has toward His Son are now directed toward every believer. After spending so much and sacrificing His Son for you, you are now number one on God's list of priorities in the universe!

There is a third insight you'll need to overcome rejection: *Just as God has now accepted you, you will have to accept others.* This is not explicitly stated in Isaiah 53, but it is very clear from Ephesians 4:32: "And be kind to one another, tenderhearted, forgiving each other, just as God in Christ also has forgiven you."

You say, "How does our acceptance before God enable us to forgive one another?" To begin with, our acceptance in the sight of God enables us to accept ourselves. During my ministry I have met scores, if not hundreds, of people who have tremendously negative thoughts about themselves. Psychologists call it a poor self-image. These people really believe that they are just awful, that they are failures. Deep inside, they consider themselves worthless. This feeling about themselves runs roughshod over their emotional responses, forcing them to react without self-assurance and confidence.

If you are one of those people, I want you to know

that you are not worth any less than any other human being. We are all of equal value in the sight of God (Acts 10:34). Your emotions are not an accurate gauge of your value.

Once you begin to see that you are accepted by God, you can say, "Lord, I thank You that You have created me. I thank You that I am alive. I thank You that You have accepted me. If You can love me and accept me just as I am, I will accept my appearance, I will accept my background, I will accept my lack of education. I will accept any negative thing that has come to me and I will say thank You, God, because one thing is sure: I am accepted and highly beloved in the sight of the Lord God." As David put it, "For my father and my mother have forsaken me, but the Lord will take me up" (Ps. 27:10).

Next, you must choose to forgive those who have wronged you. You may not feel like forgiving, but forgiveness is not an emotion. Forgiving is an act of obedience dependent on the will.

Consider the child who grows up in a home where he is rejected. One of the things he says is, "If it's the last thing I do, I'll get my parents to accept me." He works hard and is often obedient. He may do all kinds of little extra things, looking for recognition and acceptance. Unfortunately, parents are sometimes so filled with selfishness that they are unable to accept their child even with that. And if the child does achieve acceptance, it may be only temporary, based on a specific performance. That's why if your parents have rejected you and you are now an adult, the chances of you finally being accepted by them are small. It may happen, but only rarely.

The answer to your problem is not to say, "I will do anything to gain their acceptance." If you do, it can hurt your relationship with your husband or wife, damage your relationships with your children—and you merely perpetuate the rejection through another generation. You must reach the point where you simply say, "I choose to forgive them."

And what if your parents or your mate are dead? That does not matter, since you are not only doing it for their sakes. I am asking you to do it for your sake. Forgiveness is a favor you are doing yourself. Just as God has forgiven you because He chose to, you can choose to forgive a parent, a husband or wife (even an ex-husband or wife), and children who may have rejected you. I have heard of people having to go to graves and pour out their emotions so that they can finally and irrevocably choose to forgive.

Feelings are tricky. Emotions are affected by many things. So even if you have prayed to God and accepted His assessment of your worth in Christ, and even if you have deliberately chosen to forgive the one who has rejected you, the feelings may return. How do you overcome them?

Specific Actions

You can take three steps to overcome feelings of rejection. The first is to begin a life of praise. This has to become a priority. You must consistently praise the Lord because you have been accepted and highly favored of the Lord. Every day, read a psalm or two that focuses on praise to God. Thank Him for the acceptance that is secure, immovable, and not dependent on your performance. Memorize verses of praise that can be repeated when the feelings of rejection start surfacing.

Second, you must lay down all bitterness. Simply say, "Even though it hurts, and every emotion in my body militates against it, by God's grace I choose to forgive and accept the fact that Jesus bore my rejection for me so that I can be free."

Then, take the risk of making new friendships. You no longer need to be withdrawn, determined never to be hurt again. You will begin to open your life to others, making yourself vulnerable to them because you know your security ultimately does not rest in man but in God. He accepts you today just as He accepts His Son.

You have read this far and in your mind you have been saying, "That's right, but I'm afraid to get started because I might fail." God accepts even your failure. He does not reject you even after a dozen false starts. It is not three strikes and you're out. Right now you can pray the following prayer as your start.

Dear Father, I thank You that Jesus Christ died on my behalf. I thank You that He bore not only my sins, but also my sorrows. I thank You that He experienced deep rejection, and I am glad that He can identify with me. Right now I want to make the substitution; I want to make the exchange. I choose to forgive the one who has wronged me. I accept Jesus Christ's help in doing so. And because I am now highly favored, I thank You for my gifts, my limitations, and my abilities. I thank You again that I was born, and I thank You that today I can be free. Finally, because I am highly favored, I thank You that I can love others in the energy of the risen Christ. Amen.

Application

1. Based on Psalm 118:22, how did God use Christ's rejection for an ultimate good?

2. Being rejected by our parents or friends is severe, but contemplate for a moment what it would be like to be rejected by God (Matt. 8:12; Rev. 20:11-15).

3. Perhaps the best antidote for feelings of depression is to be secure in the love and acceptance of God. Memorize these promises of assurance that will focus on this relationship: Deuteronomy 32:10; Ephesians 1·3-6; 1 Peter 2:9.

4. Feelings of depression can only be overcome by a daily life of praise. Read a psalm of praise each day to God. Honor Him by expressing worship through your lips (e.g., Pss. 103; 145—50).

6

When Fear Envelops You

HAVE you ever heard someone make one of the following statements?

"I'll never drive a car in Chicago. Never! That kind of traffic scares me to death."

"I won't go with you to the banquet. I'm scared I will make a fool of myself in front of those wealthy sophisticated people."

"Don't ever ask me to say something in public. I'd be so scared that I would forget everything I wanted to say."

Or consider what a woman told me last week: "Because of a past relationship with a man, I've lived in fear for five years, afraid he'll come to the door or kill me when I go outside. So I lock myself upstairs when I'm home alone."

Fear. The kind of fear that can paralyze, that can prevent you from enjoying life, that can lock up deep inside you the gifts that God has given you, never to be used.

Some fears are normal and actually for our benefit. You are driving along the expressway and are momentarily distracted by a sign or the car next to you. When your eyes refocus on the roadway ahead, a car is entering your lane from the other side, cutting you off. A shiver of fear runs up your spine as your foot jumps onto the brake pedal.

Or you are walking with a friend down a city sidewalk. You are in a deep conversation as you approach an intersection. As you step down to the street, out of the corner of your eye you see a car approaching. With a jerk you stop and get back on the sidewalk, and as you do so a quick skip of your heartbeat reminds you that fear caused you to stop before you got out into traffic.

This kind of fear motivates you to take the children into the basement of your house when you hear that a tornado may be coming. It causes you to warn your children about the danger of playing with matches and the danger of stopping to talk to strangers.

There is a third kind of fear, a fear for which there is no logical reason. Irrational fear makes no sense to the onlooker—and usually doesn't make sense to the one afraid, either. Some people, for example, are afraid of crowds. They are fine one-on-one, but as soon as a group gathers in their area, they start to feel uncomfortable. When you ask them why they are afraid of a crowd, they often cannot explain it. Others, of course, are more comfortable in a crowd and are terrified at the idea of having to talk to someone one-on-one unless they know him very well.

Some people are afraid of marriage; others are afraid they will lose their jobs. They live with those fears year in and year out. You may be one of those afraid to go home because you keep wondering what might have happened in your absence.

Whatever your fear, remember that God created you with the capacity to fear. He built that emotional response within you just as surely as He gave you the ability to love and respond warmly to other people. Fear is part of His loving provision for us. Properly con-

trolled, fear can protect us from harm, and it can moti-
vate us to positive action. Uncontrolled fear, however,
can put us into a personal prison and stunt our personal
and spiritual growth.

The purpose of this chapter is to help you understand
and control your fear. I want to help you push back the
walls of the prison that fear has built around you so that
you can go free.

At this point you may be saying, "I don't really want
to do that. I built that wall myself to protect me from
hurt. I laid a very careful and deep foundation. I built
the walls sky high and I'm determined to live behind
them."

You may be like some people I know. They are afraid
to have company in their home. For 25 years they've
lived in their lovely home and never invited anyone
over, not even for coffee. They are afraid the water
might not boil, that the cake won't turn out right, that
their company won't like their living room decor. Something is bound to go wrong if they ever open that front
door to others. These fears are the walls they won't push
aside. In fact, their fears have become their security blanket that they hug to their bosom as tightly as Linus holds
on to his blanket.

The Apostle Paul wrote to Timothy, "For God hath
not given us the spirit of fear" (2 Tim. 1:7, KJV). And the
Apostle John reminded us that "perfect love casts out
fear" (1 John 4:18). You can be free from the bondage of
fear. Fear need not control your actions.

The paralyzing effect of fear is illustrated by an incident in Jesus' life, related in Matthew 14:22-31. Jesus had
just fed the 5,000 men, plus women and children. The
crowd was thinning out when He asked the disciples to
get into a boat and head for the other side of the lake,
where He would meet them. He went up into the mountain to pray.

When the boat was about four miles from shore, a

storm sprang up. The wind buffeted the little boat, and the waves pounded against its sides. Since many of the disciples were fishermen, this was no new experience, even though it was very dangerous. But what they saw coming across the water was definitely not normal. Walking toward them *on the water* was the figure of a man. The Scriptures record: "And when the disciples saw Him walking on the sea, they were frightened, saying, 'It is a ghost!' And they cried out for fear" (v. 26). Sound like a tough group of fishermen?

Adjusting Your Perspective

The experience of these disciples points to the first step in demolishing the walls of fear—*you must see your fear in perspective.* Matthew reported that Jesus came to those disciples, and they thought that He was a ghost. They had a fear of the storm based on experience, but their greater fear came from perceiving Jesus' figure as a ghost.

That reaction is not unusual even today. There are many who believe that when a person dies, his spirit might return to traverse the earth, haunting different places and people. You and I know this is not true; yes, there are spirits that do haunt certain people and places, but those are not human spirits. They are evil, demonic spirits. The disciples were not that spiritually perceptive yet, so when their superstitious minds focused on the advancing figure, they naturally assumed it was a ghost. They could not relate this experience to anything that had ever happened to them before, as they had never seen anyone walk on water. Only after the initial outcry caused by fear did anyone even dream that it was Jesus who was the object of their fear.

What can you learn from this about your perspective on fear? You must see that *Jesus is in the midst of your fear.* Fear has a way of distorting our perception, and we don't see and understand the true objects of our fears, but wrapped up in those objects are the loving arms and concern of Jesus Christ.

Dr. Harry Ironside used to tell a story about himself that also illustrates this point. He would pretend that he was a bear. He would get on his hands and knees and chase his son around the room, while growling like a bear. The little boy would become fearful and be really frightened at first. Then one day when the little boy was backed into a corner, he suddenly turned and rushed into his father's arms. "You're not a bear; you're my papa!" he said.

From that incident, Dr. Ironside learned an important lesson: Often the experiences we fear the most are actually acts of God. He is attempting to put His arms around us. That's why I can say with full assurance that Jesus is in the midst of your fear. The misinterpretation, the misunderstanding that has come to you as a result of that fear can be dissipated when you realize that Jesus Christ is in the midst of it—just as He was in the midst of the disciples' fear.

There is something else you must understand if you are to get the proper perspective on your fear. *Not only is Jesus Christ in the midst of your fear, but Jesus also knows what your fear is all about and the feelings it gives you.*

When Jesus came to the disciples during the fourth watch at night, He said to them, "Take courage, it is I; do not be afraid" (Matt. 14:27). I particularly like the line in the first part of the verse: "But immediately Jesus spoke to them." He recognized their fear and immediately set about allaying those fears.

What had tipped off Jesus that the disciples were afraid? Had He overheard their cries of fear? No, I'm convinced that He knew it because He is the Son of God and He knew what was troubling their hearts. There just was no way their voices could have reached Him during the high wind.

As you read this, what fear is uppermost in your

mind? What is the fear that possibly keeps you awake for part of the night, that limits your effectiveness on the job, that hampers your service for Christ? Name it—and then know that Jesus knew all along that it was there in your heart and occupying your mind.

God knew all about the fear that would consume you when He inserted the message "Fear not" more than 100 times in the Bible. You ask, "Why 100 times? Wouldn't once be enough?" Those of you who are parents of preschool children probably know why. My wife and I have had to tell our children some things at least 100 times! Why? Because we have learned that sometimes even 99 times are not enough. And God said "Fear not" over 100 times because He knows what is going on inside of us. He knows that when we are paralyzed by fear we don't hear very well.

Adjusting Your Focus

Before we go on to the second step in overcoming our fears, let's summarize the first: To deal with fear, you must get a proper perspective on your fear, and that happens only when you recognize that Jesus is in the midst of it and knows all about your fear. This then leads us to the second step—*you must have the right focus during your fear.*

Let's examine Peter's experience with Christ. Jesus said as He approached the boat, "It is I" (Matt. 14:27). To this Peter quickly responded, "Lord, if it is You, command me to come to You on the water" (v. 28). He was ready for a quick test of the authenticity of that voice and Person.

Some people are like that. They are never sure whether God means what He says and they always want to test it out. That can be dangerous, for the Bible says, "You shall not put the Lord your God to the test" (Deut. 6:16). Yet in this instance, Peter did risk the test and said, "If it is You"—implying that he wasn't quite sure yet—"command me to come to You on the water."

Jesus said, "Come!" (v. 29)

When Jesus said that word, Peter should have rested in the absolute assurance from the Lord Himself that he could make it to His Master. Jesus wasn't about to say "Come" and let Peter sink. Yet Peter's focus shifted from Jesus to the wind, and that resulted in more fear despite the invitation from the Lord Himself.

Our focus should never be on circumstances. When Peter began walking on the water, he was on solid ground with the Lord. The Bible says he "came toward Jesus," implying his eyes were on Jesus (v. 29). When his eyes shifted focus and he saw the waves, he also felt and heard the wind that was so boisterous. At that moment, "he became afraid" and began to sink (v. 30).

Like a lot of us, Peter had within him the alternating spirits of fear and trust. When he looked at the Lord, he trusted. When he looked at his circumstances, he became afraid. Focusing on his circumstances made Peter doubt his ability to negotiate the distance between himself and Jesus. That word *doubt* means to try to go both ways, and that was what Peter was trying to do.

Instead of focusing on the circumstances, your focus must be on God's promises. Jesus had, in effect, promised Peter that he would be able to walk on the water and make it all the way to Jesus. Peter should have focused on that promise and kept walking, regardless of the wind and waves. He did not do it and started sinking as fear of the wind took hold in his heart.

Focusing on God's promises means that we are obedient to the call of God in them. We choose to obey despite the fears that might arise from circumstances. Let's suppose your problem is fear of crowds. You simply feel uncomfortable as soon as more than half a dozen people are gathered together. Let's further suppose you are paralyzed by that fear. Determined to overcome that fear, no matter what, you decide to go into that crowd, saying inside yourself, "I will overcome this fear; I will overcome this fear." Do you think fear will flee as the crowd begins engulfing you?

Certainly not, because your whole focus is on your fear, and the minute you get into that crowd, that fear will again come upon you. It will arise like the mist at dawn and envelop your heart, and you'll rush out of that crowd, totally defeated.

On the other hand, your focus can be on obedience. You can say to yourself, "God in His Word has commanded me to get together with His people, and this fear is hindering me from doing that. So I will focus on Jesus Christ and His promises and move in obedience to Him. If I happen to become afraid in a crowd, and I'm hoping I won't, I will simply have to live with it. I will accept it because it has happened before and I have lived through it. I will be obedient regardless of my feelings of fear." If you do that, you will soon discover that your attention will shift away from your fears. Soon you will be able to be in crowds, preoccupied with your responsibility to interact with others and love them as Christ commanded. In time, those fears will not trouble you anymore.

The reason for this is both psychological and spiritual. The psychological reason is that when we focus on the very thing we are trying to get rid of, its power over us actually increases. In this case, fear becomes a self-fulfilling prophecy. If you focus on how afraid you are, you will soon discover that you are very much afraid—indeed, your fear will grow stronger. But if your focus is on Jesus and on your obedience to Him, His power will flow through your whole being and help drive away the fear.

If Peter had kept his eyes on Jesus, he would have been able to walk across the Atlantic Ocean as long as Jesus had said, "Come." Perfect love casts out fear, and it does so because your love for God and His promises transcends the fear and overcomes that crippling force in your spiritual life.

Consider the woman who is afraid of dogs. One day when she hears a dog snarl, she remembers that her one-year-old is outside playing. Without a doubt she will rush outside, grab the child, and run back inside even if the dog comes at her. Her love is stronger than her fear. How much more is loving obedience to God able to overcome paralyzing fear!

I truly feel sorry for people who live in a constant state of fear. They are forever taking their spiritual temperatures to see how much fear they have. Focusing on their fears only increases those fears. They should throw away the thermometer and begin basking in the glow of God's warm love, for it will cast out fear.

The Step of Faith

Yet the experience of Peter and the disciples that night reminds us of another step in overcoming fear. To be truly victorious over fear, you need not only the right perspective on your fear and a proper focus, *but you also need to take a step of faith.*

Notice what Jesus did when Peter cried out in his fear, "Lord, save me!" Jesus stretched out His hand and took hold of Peter before he had gone down very far. Then He said, "O you of little faith, why did you doubt?" (v. 31) Jesus pointedly referred to the real reason for Peter's failure, his lack of faith.

Let me remind you of what you must believe. First, you must recognize that God ordains fearful circumstances. "Hold it," you're saying, "run that by me again." OK, why were the disciples in the boat in the middle of a dangerous storm at the fourth watch of the night? *They were there because Jesus had told them to get into the boat and cross the lake ahead of Him.* They received explicit instructions and obeyed. Yet despite that they found themselves in the middle of a storm.

As lovingly as I can, let me remind you that the smoothest path in life is not always the most holy path. Sometimes the most holy path is the roughest path. Some of you are probably saying, "Right on. I gave up my job for Jesus Christ. I could be earning more money, but I believe God has called me into a ministry for Him. So now we are having financial problems in our family. We are experiencing health problems on top of everything, even though we believe we obeyed God." That was exactly the experience of Jesus' disciples—circumstances were difficult even though they were doing the will of God!

Jesus wants you to understand that no matter how severe the storm, it is God-ordained. And because He ordained it, He is there in it with you. Once you recognize that, you will, like the disciples, worship in reverence and in awe at the power that is active in your life.

Of course, sometimes we bring difficulties on ourselves, particularly when we consciously disobey God. But even then God wants us to learn from our failures. Consequences become the means of God's discipline. Yet He is there with us just the same.

Secondly, God not only ordains fearful circumstances; we can be grateful that He also monitors them—that is, He keeps close watch on how we are faring in the midst of life's storms. Though the disciples couldn't see Christ when the storm began, He could see them! Isn't that true of our experiences? Often we wonder where Christ is or whether He has lost interest in our predicaments. But He is on the sidelines, watching the whole ordeal. And when push comes to shove, as it so often does in life, I would prefer that Christ see me rather than I see Him!

Christ carefully watched the situation and came to them in their distress. He calculated the best time to come to them personally. It happened to be 3 A.M., the darkest hour of the night. No sooner nor any later did Christ choose to make His appearance. The disciples, exhausted by the storm and frustrated by Christ's apparent indifference to their plight, had come to the end of their rope—Christ met them there (and calmed the storm [v. 32], even though His appearance was initially more frightening than the storm).

Where are you in your battle with fear? Is the evening turning to darkness, or is the darkness already beginning to blend into the morning light? Wherever, I want you to remember that Christ is near, taking inventory of your situation and available when you turn to Him. His timing is perfect, His love intense. The psalmist wrote, "I sought the Lord, and He answered me, and delivered me from all my fears" (Ps. 34:4). Like the disciples, this man came to worship the God who delivered him from his fears.

Let me be clear: Learning to focus on God's promises in faith does not mean that God will always change the fearful circumstances. Sometimes the storms of life continue; often those fearful situations rear their ugly heads once again. But though the circumstances might not change, we will. We will live without those paralyzing fears that rob us of our Christian freedom.

Finally, in the Scriptures there is a direct connection between God's presence and the absence of fear. For example, Hebrews 13:5-6 implies that we can be free from the fear of poverty and the fear of men by remembering that God is with us: "Let your way of life be free from the love of money, being content with what you have; for He Himself has said, 'I will never desert you, nor will I ever forsake you,' so that we confidently say, 'The Lord is my Helper, I will not be afraid. What shall man do to me?'" We can be content with our possessions and free from the fear of men because God will never abandon us. We've always got Him beside us.

The circumstances that we fear remind me of the walls in a penitentiary in British Columbia, Canada. When the structure was being demolished, the workmen discovered something interesting. Though the gates were steel and the windows were barred, the outer walls were made only of woodboard covered with clay and paper, painted to look as if the walls were thick metal. Anyone could have gone through those walls with little effort, but no prisoner ever tried it; they all believed the walls could never budge.

You will find that your fears are much the same; the walls you have built may appear formidable. You may even feel comfortable in your prison and find the thought of freedom frightening.

But today, you can push down those walls in the name of Jesus Christ. In your fears you can see the face of Jesus Christ disguised; you can choose to memorize God's promises rather than catering to your fluctuating emotions. You can accept the storms of life as God's will, His plan for strengthening your faith. You can join Peter in stepping out of the boat and walking with Christ. The circumstances that threaten to be over your head will suddenly be under your feet!

You'll have the exhilaration of stepping onto a cloud and discovering that your feet are on solid rock. Christ has already conquered your fears. Are you ready to accept His victory?

Application

1. What consequences may fear have in a person's life? (Lev. 26:36; Matt. 26:69-75; 28:4; Luke 21:26; John 9:22; 19:12-16)

2. Notice how our fear of man should be replaced by our fear of God (Ps. 27:1; Prov. 10:27; Matt. 10:26-31). Why are the two kinds of fear mutually exclusive?

3. If it is never God's will for us to be overcome with fear (2 Tim. 1:7), what might be the source of our fears? What did God do for David? (Ps. 34:4)

4. Satan often exploits our fears, telling us we must live in our private prisons. Why do we have the author-

ity to command our fears to leave us? (Read Eph. 1:15—2:6.)

5. Think of all the fears you have had that were unfounded. How can we prevent such a waste of nervous energy in the future? (1 Peter 5:7)

6. Perhaps man's greatest fear is the fear of death. What can we learn from Christ and Paul about how to approach the experience? (Luke 23:46; John 13:1, 5; 2 Tim. 4:6-8) Find other passages that tell us how believers have faced death in the past—Stephen, for example.

7

Loneliness: The Quest for Companionship

T.S. ELIOT wrote, "Hell is oneself; Hell is alone, the other figures in it merely projections."

Millions of people suffer from the distress of isolation, the feeling that no one really knows them and even worse, no one cares. They are tormented by the crushing thought that they are alone *in their world*.

For most of us loneliness is a temporary feeling, but for many it is a continual experience; it's the experience of dying by the inch. "To feel lonely is to feel disconnected. For those who have difficulty in starting a close relationship, it is felt as the *lack* of being wanted and belonging" (Craig Ellison, *Loneliness, the Search for Intimacy*, Christian Herald Books, p. 27).

Why Are People Lonely?
There are several reasons for loneliness and we shall list some of the more common ones.

1. *The loneliness of rejection.* Consider a woman whose father or marriage partner refuses to respond to her desire for communication and love; or perhaps there was favoritism in the family and someone else received all the attention. This woman might experience a sense of

worthlessness which leads to self-pity, and self-pity begets despair, and despair triggers withdrawal. She feels isolated, unable to form new friendships. Craig Ellison reports a study which showed that the most lonely people are those who were unsure about their parents' love (*Loneliness, the Search for Intimacy*, p. 25). Their feelings of distrust and rejection prevent them from forming intimate relationships.

A loner who stays on the fringes of the crowd only continues to multiply the psychological distance between himself and other people. When everyone else is enjoying the party, he walks back to his apartment—alone. Once again his rejection is confirmed.

In fact, shyness often results from being put down by others; it is symptomatic of a feeling of unworthiness. The shy person fears further rejection and would rather remain silent than make an inappropriate remark.

The problem of rejection is accentuated by the crass indifference of society toward those who are physically or emotionally isolated. When I visited a nursing home several years ago, I asked one of the supervisors, "How many of the residents of this home are visited by relatives at least several times a year?" She replied that only about 30 percent receive such visits. Seventy percent have no one to visit them, even at Christmas.

Children have no idea of how deeply they may be wounding their parents because of indifference. One woman I know had two daughters who had not contacted her in 10 years. They were angry, and would not respond to any overtures their mother made. The grief and loneliness were almost too great for the mother to bear.

2. *The loneliness of separation.* Moving from one location to another can be painful emotionally. We can't bear the thought of leaving our dearest friends to go to a city where we know no one. We are convinced that *no one* can take the place of our former friends. For the first few

months in the new city we sulk, bemoaning our loneliness.

Even more traumatic is the separation caused by death. The permanence of that separation—the fact that we'll never see the person again—makes the world appear cruel. Every piece of furniture in the room reminds the survivor of the loss suffered and sharply intensifies the loneliness. Some people feel God is unjust to let them stay alive when their life's partner is gone.

Several years ago a single engine plane crashed soon after take-off from Meigs Field in Chicago. The pilot survived, but his wife and children were killed. A few days later the man committed suicide and left a note, "My wife and children need me, I've got to leave and be with them."

For some people, divorce causes similar feelings of hurt and desolation. There's no one to talk to; no one to share joys and sorrows . . . no one to discuss matters that are important. Loneliness actually feeds on itself and magnifies all tragedies.

Such people must be told that eventually life will resume the semblance of normality. People do pull out of the depression of separation. It may take weeks or even months, but there can be healing and rebuilding.

3. *The loneliness of non-intimacy.* Many marriage partners are lonely when there is little communication in the home. But loneliness is a special problem for single adults. In our churches and society, singles don't seem to fit in very well. Yet, it is estimated that 17 million adults live alone. Faced with an empty apartment, they must cook their own meals and make their own plans. There's no one to talk to; no one to discuss the problems of the day. No one to go to bed with.

The frustration of sexual desires causes some singles to develop sexual relationships which may or may not result in future marriage. Actually, such a solution to loneliness eventually compounds the problem: now there is not only the feeling of being alone, but the added emotion of guilt and the diminishing of one's self-worth.

Most singles dread holidays, particularly Christmas. It's a time to reflect back to childhood when life was carefree and happy . . . and when the family was together. It's hard to have such memories facing the stark reality of the present. Also, there is the added perception that everyone else is enjoying the warmth and security of family gatherings, but the single person feels left out. What is a time of joy for some is a time of depression for others.

4. *The loneliness of sin.* The root cause of loneliness is *sin*. In the Garden of Eden sin not only built a barrier between Adam and Eve and God, but also between Adam and Eve themselves. God created them as social creatures who would have their needs met through both spiritual and physical relationships. But the freedom of their fellowship was interrupted with the guilt and fear of sin.

After they sinned, Adam and Eve became self-centered and corrupt. The sins which grew out of that initial act of disobedience continued to divide men and women from one another. Consider for a moment the works of the flesh mentioned in Galatians 5:19-21. Each of these causes personal alienation and disrupts our relationships with other members of the human family.

Adam and Eve tried to excuse themselves from guilt, much like modern man who is quite convinced that he can handle his sin apart from the Cross. But as Craig Ellison points out, "The price for maintaining ego-defenses is loneliness. When we can no longer allow ourselves to be known as we really are because what we are is shameful, we are faced with a basic difficulty in bridging the gap between. We cannot understand ourselves, and we often feel misunderstood" (*Loneliness, the Search for Intimacy*, p. 50).

After Cain killed Abel, he was banished from his parents and was a fugitive on the earth. His loneliness compounded his guilt, which he said was "greater than I can bear" (Gen. 4:13, KJV). He, along with all of the descendants of Adam and Eve, was now suspicious, distrustful of future relationships. Psychological walls and emotional barriers were found everywhere.

Is there a way out of loneliness? There would not be, if it were not possible to reestablish ruptured relationships. But God has not left us without an escape from our alienation. The sense of belonging which we desperately need for our emotional sanity can be found even in our fallen world.

How Can We Overcome Loneliness?

People will do all kinds of things to escape loneliness. Witness the proliferation of singles' bars, discos, and singles' communities. One of the more creative approaches was by a man who went to a psychiatrist and asked for a split personality. At least that way he would have someone to live with!

Seriously, it is necessary for us to face ourselves honestly and begin right *where we are* in becoming rightly related with God and people. Such a transformation is possible. Indeed, God invites us to be reconciled to Himself. This provides the basis for other friendships.

1. *Reestablish our relationship with God.* Yes, sin destroys our fellowship with God, but Christ's death on the cross means that the barriers have been dismantled. In other words, we can be cleansed from our guilt and shame so that we can be rightly related to God once again.

Look at it this way: On the cross, Christ made a payment for sin that necessitated His own separation from God the Father. When He cried out, "My God, My God, why hast Thou forsaken Me?" (Matt. 27:46), it was because He was experiencing the most excruciating loneliness imaginable—isolation from God the Father.

But because Christ was willing to bear our separation

from God, we can be reconciled to Him. Christ assured His disciples, "If anyone loves Me, he will keep My Word; and My Father will love him, and We will come to him, and make Our abode with him" (John 14:23). Christ's rejection makes our acceptance by God possible. Sin is removed when we believe in Christ's work for us.

Remember Jacob's first night away from home? He had left feeling guilty because he had wronged his brother. He also felt grieved because he would be separated from his mother for a long time. He was his mother's favorite son, and now he was leaving her with his aged and blind father Isaac.

But that night, the Lord appeared to Jacob and said, "And behold, I am with you, and will keep you wherever you go, and will bring you back to this land; for I will not leave you until I have done what I have promised you" (Gen. 28:15).

Jacob was traveling alone. He was defenseless against attack by a marauding band of desert dwellers. He had no guide to show him the best route to take. When he got to his destination, he would be among strangers, even though they were his relatives. With that prospect ahead of him, God's promise that He would keep Jacob wherever he would go was most reassuring.

This is the God who comes to us in our loneliness. He is aware of the pain of separation from loved ones, the loneliness of not knowing what the future holds. He is even aware of the guilt we may be trying to deny. He comes to us and says, "Behold, I am with you."

When Jacob awoke he said, "Surely the Lord is in this place, and I did not know it" (v. 16). He was so afraid of what he had dreamed, that he continued by exclaiming, "How awesome is this place! This is none other than the house of God, and this is the gate of heaven" (v. 17).

So Jacob learned that God is near. He was always there; everywhere at the same time. In fact, God was there long before Jacob found the stone for his pillow.

But Jacob did not recognize that God was close to him until after his dream. Jacob's own moral failure, his sense of guilt, made him think that God was far away. Sometimes because of our own sense of worthlessness we ask, "Where is God?" But in reality He is beside us all the time. No matter how far you may *feel* you are from God, He is with you all the time. Like Jacob, the distance between us and God is not physical or geographical; it is moral.

Sometimes I liken this moral separation to radio waves. We cannot see them or feel them. Yet they totally fill the air around us. In fact, they are in us. Yet we do not become aware of them until we tune in a radio that translates them into a wavelength we can understand. In the same way, God is with you, beside you, but you may not always be in fellowship with Him. You may be on a different frequency.

How do we get on His wavelength? The Bible is very clear that we must confess our sins. When we do, God will forgive us and cleanse us from all unrighteousness (1 John 1:9). When we obey and accept God's Word by faith, we can be assured of His presence.

When Jacob awoke and recognized God's presence with him, he exclaimed, "How awesome is this place! This is none other than the house of God, and this is the gate of heaven" (Gen. 28:17). Because of Christ, a lonely apartment can also be a house of God; it can be the gate of heaven.

I've visited Christians in lonely hospital rooms only to find that they were enjoying the presence of God there. When I visited Dr. William Culbertson, who was President of Moody Bible Institute for many years, I was with him for only a few precious moments. Yet when I stopped at the nurses' station, one of them said, "When you go into that man's room, it is as if you are walking into the presence of God." Yes, despite all its loneliness and terrifying consequences, the hospital room can become the house of God, the gate of heaven.

About 1,500 years after Jacob's experience, a man sat under a fig tree, meditating on the Scriptures. Perhaps he was thinking of the story of Jacob when Philip arrived and announced, "We have found Him of whom Moses in the Law and also the Prophets wrote" (John 1:45). Nathanael listened to Philip and responded somewhat disdainfully, "Can any good thing come out of Nazareth?" (v. 46) Philip replied in effect, "See for yourself."

When Christ saw Nathanael He said, "Behold an Israelite indeed, in whom is no guile!" (v. 47) Instantly Nathanael knew that Christ had read his thoughts. Nathanael blurted out, "Rabbi, You are the Son of God; You are the King of Israel" (v. 49). Then Christ answered, "Truly, truly I say to you, you shall see the heavens opened, and the angels of God ascending and descending upon the Son of man" (v. 51). Obviously, Christ was alluding to Jacob's dream.

The ladder becomes symbolic of God's blessings brought to us through Jesus Christ. The angels of God ascend and descend upon Christ . . . just as our worship ascends to God and His blessings descend to us. Christ is the ladder who joins man and God. Any room, any territory, no matter how isolated, can thus become the house of God and the gate of heaven!

Just think of the strength of God that some people have experienced in their loneliness. In George Bernard Shaw's play, *St. Joan*, Joan asks, "Do you think you can frighten me by telling me that I am alone? France is alone; and God is alone; and what is my loneliness before the loneliness of my country and my God? . . . Well, my loneliness shall be my strength too: It is better to be alone with God: His friendship will not fail me, nor His counsel, nor His love. In His strength I will dare, and dare, and dare, until I die" (Scene V).

God is as near to you as the air you breathe and fellowship with Him can be restored when you receive the forgiveness Christ died to give you. Loneliness is God's invitation for you and He to become better acquainted.

2. *Reestablish a relationship with people.* Loneliness is a time for self-evaluation and reflection. We have to think about our priorities and our own personalities as well. "Why don't I form friendships easily?" That's a question that many people should ponder. And here's another, "Might I be driving other people away by my own attitudes and actions?" For example, no one wants to become intimate with a person who is bitter, angry, or willfully self-centered. Some people are such an emotional drain to others that they only invite further rejection and more loneliness.

What about this question, "Am I prepared to become sacrificially involved in the lives of others?" Once again, motives are important. It's not a matter of self-giving in order that we may get; some people try too hard to make friends and smother their acquaintances with excessive demands.

All friendships involve risk; there is a possibility that we may be betrayed or become disappointed in those whom we befriend. But without such risks there are no rewards. We must be willing to build bridges and to gently put our emotional weight upon them. We'll find that making friends is satisfying . . . the process will satisfy our social needs.

Specifically, how can we learn to make friends? And what barriers have to be crossed to pay the price of satisfying relationships? Here are some appropriate considerations.

Identify any guilt that may be preventing you from forming close friendships. Perhaps you are experiencing false guilt, like the widow who thinks that she cannot enjoy the company of others without minimizing her love for her deceased husband. Or perhaps you feel guilty because of past failures and even though God has forgiven you, you've not forgiven yourself.

Memories have their place, but we cannot be bound to them. The reason that Christ died was so the past would not control us.

Perhaps you feel like a failure and therefore are uncomfortable in the presence of others who seem to be more successful than you. Once again you must bring yourself to the Cross to be assured that God accepts you fully. Convinced of that, you can begin to make friends. You'll discover that there are hundreds of people just like you who are fearful and who believe that they have failed so miserably that no one could ever befriend them again. There's someone out there who is waiting to meet you.

3. *Identify any bitterness that makes you withdrawn and aloof.* If you've been hurt, you may not want to risk another friendship. But in reacting negatively, you are forestalling the healing process that needs to begin. God may take some people out of your life, but He replaces them with others. If you are resentful, you will always be emotionally crippled and your friendships will fall short of the honesty and openness needed to meet your social needs. Confess that bitterness to God and trust Him to use you in becoming acquainted with others.

4. *Your self-pity can lead to social isolation.* You may be thinking, *Why did this awful thing happen to me?* The more time you spend alone nursing your own wounds, the more likely you will be opening those wounds. Actually, being alone is seldom the answer to an emotional need. The author of the *Devil's Advocate* wrote, "It is no new thing to be lonely. It comes to all of us sooner or later. . . . If we try to retreat from it, we end in a darker hell. . . . But if we face it, if we remember that there are a million others like us, if we try to reach out to comfort them and not ourselves, we find in the end we are lonely no longer" (*Loneliness, the Search for Intimacy*, p. 163).

5. *Forgo activities that foster isolation rather than build relationships.* Television programs and even reading materi-

al (especially material that exploits your fantasies) can make you retreat into your inner world. As a result, you hang a sign on your heart that reads NO ENTRANCE.

I'm amazed at the number of lonely people who feed their loneliness through the activities they choose. Sometimes I think they *want* to be lonely. Though they may be complaining about their plight, they have determined to avoid social contacts that would integrate them into the Christian community.

6. *Seek out those whom you are able to help and befriend.* Don't expect people to come to you; you must go to them. I've known people who were physically handicapped and yet in some way they gave themselves to the legitimate needs of those around them and formed friendships. Such activity practically guarantees that we will be free from depression because the Scriptures assure us, "And if you give yourself to the hungry, and satisfy the desire of the afflicted, then your light will rise in darkness, and your gloom will become like midday" (Isa. 58:10).

7. *Focus on Scripture passages that promise that you are able to make friends and that remind you of God's concern for your hospitality toward others (Luke 14:7-15).* You must make a conscious effort to include others in your world. God will reward you generously as you obey Him.

I heard a story about some soldiers in France who brought the body of a dead comrade to a cemetery for burial. The priest told them that it was a Roman Catholic cemetery and unless their friend had been baptized and brought up in the Catholic church, he could not be buried there. The soldiers reluctantly admitted that he was not a Catholic. So they buried him on the other side of the fence just outside of the cemetery.

The next day the soldiers returned to check on the grave of their comrade and to their dismay they couldn't find it! As they were about to leave, the priest met them and explained that he was deeply troubled by his refusal to have their friend buried in the cemetery. So early in the morning, he had moved the fence a few paces so that the body of the comrade would be within the cemetery gates.

I'm not using this story to illustrate the need of an ecumenical approach to Christian unity, but it illustrates what we all should be doing: moving the fences we've built around us to include others within our world. Loneliness will then vanish and we will feel whole once again.

Application

1. List all the reasons why it is possible to be lonely in a crowd.

2. What do we learn about God's provision for our companionship in Genesis 2:18? What provision ought the church make for those who are presently unmarried?

3. Many people are lonely because they've been hurt. They do not want to risk further friendships. What can we do to help them overcome such fears?

4. Perhaps the most severe loneliness is that caused by rejection. Often, those who need friendship the most are rejected because of their personality, appearance, or lack of social graces. Specifically, what should we do to give such people a sense of identity and a feeling that they belong?

5. To what extent can friendship with God meet our need for companionship? Consider Christ's repeated reference to His Father's presence (John 8:16-19).

8

Controlling Anger

WE all know that Alexander the Great conquered the world. But what few people know is that this mighty general could not conquer himself!

Cletus, a dear friend of Alexander's and a general in his army, became intoxicated and ridiculed the emperor in front of his men. Blinded by anger, quick as lightning, Alexander snatched a spear from the hand of a soldier and hurled it at Cletus. Though he had only intended to scare the drunken general, his aim was true and the spear took the life of his childhood friend.

Deep remorse followed his anger. Overcome with guilt, Alexander tried to take his own life with the same spear, but he was stopped by his men. For days he lay sick calling for his friend Cletus, chiding himself as a murderer.

Alexander the Great conquered many cities; he conquered many countries, but he failed miserably to conquer his own spirit. If Alexander was unable to conquer anger, can we?

When resentments, frustrations, hurt feelings, and simple fatigue accumulate, we explode. Is such anger always wrong, sometimes wrong—or maybe even sometimes right? Is there actually a time to get good and angry? Why did Paul remind us, "Be angry, and yet do not sin; do not let the sun go down on your anger and do not give the devil an opportunity"? (Eph. 4:26-27)

By now some of you are ready to tune me out or to read on only because you might be able to help a friend. You're saying, "I never get angry like that!" I'm not sure I should believe you—I am not convinced you are that dead! Maybe that's because I have a temper, an admission that may surprise some. More to the point is that God gets angry as well. We read in Psalm 7:11, "God is angry with the wicked every day" (KJV).

You say that is a different kind of anger. So did I, and I was convinced that God would have to reach down and change my emotional structure so I would never have those feelings of anger again. But I was wrong, and now I am glad God did not change my emotional makeup. When I realized that God becomes angry, I realized that anger as such is not sinful. Over and over again you read that God was angry with the people of Israel, that the anger of the Lord burned against them.

God's anger is not confined to the Old Testament, however. In Mark 3:5 we read that Jesus Christ went into the synagogue and "looked round about on them with anger" (KJV). Stop for a moment and imagine the scene. Jesus went into that synagogue on the Sabbath and noticed a man with a withered hand—probably the man was planted there by the religious leaders to see what Jesus would do. Would He heal him on the Sabbath? Jesus, reading their minds, asked, "Is it lawful to do good on the Sabbath days, or to do evil? To save life, or to kill?" (Mark 3:4, KJV) Their silence gave Him the answer, an answer that genuinely angered Him because it revealed the hardness of their hearts.

So we see that God the Father was angry, and God the Son became angry. Another Old Testament passage shows how the third Person in the Godhead can be in-

volved. When the Ammonites surrounded the city of Jabesh-gilead and appeared strong enough to take the city,
the city fathers volunteered to make a covenant with the
Ammonites. They would become their servants. But Na-
hash, the Ammonite leader, demanded the right to put
out the right eyes of the residents of the city before making peace. The elders of the city pleaded for time and
sent out messengers to the rest of Israel, asking for help.
When Saul heard this, "the Spirit of God came upon
Saul . . . and he became very angry" (1 Sam. 11:6). That
anger resulted in the deliverance of the people in the city
of Jabesh-gilead.

Clearly, anger in itself is not sin; it is not evil. Anger is
found within the Godhead; it is also part of being human. God made us with the capacity for emotional responses, and we cannot and need not prevent those
emotions from welling up.

As with so many areas of human experience, the Bible
does provide a warning signal. Under the inspiration of
the Holy Spirit, Paul wrote that we are not to sin when
we get angry, indicating the very real possibility of sin
when the emotional response of anger occurs.

The Apostle Paul suggested that anger can be a real
problem when he told the Ephesians, "Do not let the
sun go down on your anger" (Eph. 4:26). Anger that
persists beyond sundown is uncontrolled, and it is
uncontrolled anger that causes our problems. It ruptures
relationships, it stifles spiritual growth, it gives place to
the devil (v. 27), and it opens the door to sinning.

Consider the carefully nourished relationship between
a man and a woman during courtship and early marriage. There is good communication. One day a problem
arises. The disagreement becomes so sharp that things
get out of hand, and words are flung at each other like
poison-tipped arrows. Later the husband can say that he
is sorry, and the wife can say she is sorry. They forgive
each other. At least they *say* they do. Yet both know

something has happened to their relationship. There is something that cannot be regained because of the hurt. The relationship has experienced a rupture, and it may never grow together the way it once was.

Think of children growing up with deeply wounded spirits because of the unfairness of parents exercising discipline when extremely angry. It is not wrong to discipline children in anger, but it is wrong to discipline them when anger is out of control. Then the discipline becomes an emotional explosion instead of a corrective action growing out of love for the child. The resulting fracture in the parent-child relationship may widen during the rebellious teen years, and then concerned parents wonder, "What went wrong?"

Uncontrolled anger does not only affect others. It can stifle your spiritual growth because it builds a sense of guilt and results in discouragement. I've known men who put a fist through the wall in a fit of anger. They then cried to the Lord in their feelings of guilt, asking for deliverance. They wanted deliverance because they wanted to be spared the embarrassment of doing something foolish.

Many times such explosions of anger are merely a symptom of unresolved problems. The explosion is like the tip of the iceberg, revealing only a little of the submerged anger. Such people may be angry at life itself, or they may be angry at their marriage partner, their children, or God Himself. At the least provocation, their anger flames up uncontrolled. The sense of guilt felt by such people only fuels the anger.

Under such conditions, it is not surprising that uncontrolled anger gives place to the devil. That is clearly what Paul implied when he wrote in Ephesians 4:27 that we are not to give place to the devil. Uncontrolled anger gives place to the devil because of the thoughts revealed by the torrent of words in such moments—and often by our irrational behavior.

With that experience as a wedge, the devil then whispers words of discouragement, of hopelessness. All the other weapons in his arsenal are quickly marshaled, and unless the Christian recognizes what is going on and seeks forgiveness from the Lord and others involved, Satan will have a field day. No wonder the Scriptures indicate that anger is closely related to demonic activity.

Hard to believe? Not really, when you see people throwing things in anger, putting their feet or fists through walls. I've known people who attempted to track down the root of such anger and discovered it started after they dabbled in some occult practices and attended seances.

The potential for sinning is revealed when we examine the way people handle anger. Some people admit, "I just blow up." Others express it less dramatically: "I just give him a piece of my mind." Actually, most of us cannot afford to do that—that's why we read in the Book of Proverbs that the discreet person is slow to anger (Prov. 16:32). Some people tell us we will "feel better" when we blow up, but in the process we say and do things that are better left unsaid and undone.

Nor can I recommend handling anger the way some psychologists suggest. They say we should take a pillow and pretend that the pillow is the object of our anger: our mother, wife, husband, child, or employer. Then we are to really pound the pillow until we feel better. Unfortunately, that merely fuels our anger and provides no permanent release. It certainly is not the biblical way of handling anger.

A less destructive way of handling anger is to clam up. Such people know that an angry explosion will result in ruptured relationships, so they say, "I'd rather not say anything." Instead they seethe, like Mount St. Helens in Washington. They may or may not blow up occasionally. Even if they don't, their failure to communicate also damages relationships. Clamming up is definitely not a biblical way of handling anger, for it is a refusal to face the issues that God wants a person to face. This stunts growth in relationships, does not resolve tensions, and will probably result in physical symptoms that seem unexplainable.

The life of Nehemiah provides a beautiful example of how to control anger. Nehemiah had come back to Jerusalem from a fine position in the court of Artaxerxes to supervise the rebuilding of the walls of Jerusalem. A delegation of Hebrews had come with him, and I suspect some had come because of the opportunities to make an extra shekel during such a period of progress. These and local opportunists had used a period of scarcity to claim both fields and daughters from those who owed them money.

The Need for Honesty

When Nehemiah became aware of what was going on he wrote, "I was very angry when I had heard their outcry" (Neh. 5:6). Now that's the kind of anger I appreciate and would encourage. I wish that we had people today who could get angry at the sort of programs seen on television, at the violence and child abuse in homes. I would like to see more people become angry at the child neglect in our country, at the social injustice, at racial discrimination—and begin to do some things about them. Jesus did when He ridded the temple of those who were defiling it by getting rich on dishonest gain.

Nehemiah's anger resulted in positive action. Notice the steps. First, *he admitted he was angry.* He wrote it down for all of us to become aware of it. Praise God for someone who can admit to being angry!

A preacher friend tells of the time in a deacon's meeting when one of the men pounded his fist on the table and glared at those around it in obvious anger. When admonished he said, "What do you mean? I'm not angry." He refused to admit his anger. He's like the person who says that he's forgiven so-and-so and then hands you a list of the offenses forgiven. The list might as well have been written in concrete.

Nehemiah could have said, "I'll let sleeping dogs lie." But if he had done that, the whole place would have been filled with sleeping dogs! Instead he said, "I was very angry," and in the following verses we see how he could be both good and angry.

The Need for a Solution

In verse 7, the Bible reveals that *Nehemiah consulted with himself.* He thought things through before he opened his mouth. He did not let Satan drive a wedge in his relationship with the people by saying the first thing he thought of.

Consider how this applies in a marriage relationship. Many times a legitimate issue is being discussed at the wrong time. A man works hard to earn the money to provide for his family. The wife works hard to keep the house, prepare the food, and look after the children. All day long, the husband's been thinking about the race car he and his friends are building. He promises himself that as soon as supper is over, he'll get with his friends and forget the boredom of his job. He comes home, gives his wife a peck on the cheek, makes sure Johnny gets away from the television and to the supper table, eats his meal, and heads for the door.

About this time, the pent-up frustration of the weary wife surfaces.

"There you go again. You're so selfish. You never think of anyone but yourself!"

Suddenly the husband feels guilty about what he has looked forward to all day. Yet he has promised his friends, and not to go would mean disappointing them and losing face. He slams the door and heads for his car.

Understand, the wife is probably right. But that is the wrong time to throw that accusation at him. At that moment, the wife needs to "consult" with herself and ask the Lord for wisdom to bring up the issue at the right time, for there is clearly a problem.

"Hey," you say, "I am one of those who gets so overwhelmed by my emotions that there is no way under the sun I will be able to control my anger in a situation like that." Really? I am sure you remember a time when you were in the middle of a heated argument and the telephone rang. You walked over to the phone and said "Hello" in the friendliest of voices. After the conversation, your argument continued where it left off.

Why were you able to be so calm on the phone? Obviously, you wanted to impress your friend and didn't want him to know you were in the middle of a fit of anger. The same is true when you get angry at your boss.

I remember a professor at the university who really upset me. I could cheerfully have told him off in no uncertain terms, but I did not. And I am glad I did not, for it would have ruptured our relationship, and in many ways I respect him highly.

Amazingly, we seem to hurt most those who are closest to us. We have so much respect for our boss that we won't tell him off. Yet we explode at our wife or husband, the person we promised to love and cherish.

James gives us a comparison between the tongue and a little rudder that can steer a large ship. Yes, a small rudder can control a large ship; so the tongue controls the whole body. According to James, if we do not "stumble" in what we say, we are able to bridle the whole body as well. That's a man of discipline! Yet James also makes it clear that "no one can tame the tongue" by himself (3:8). That is why the Bible lists self-control as part of the fruit of the Spirit (Gal. 5:23).

Nehemiah "consulted with himself" to gain control of his thoughts before he expressed his anger. I have found that a simple thing like counting to 20 can help tremendously in putting my thoughts into low gear and helping to control my tongue.

The Need for Communication

Once Nehemiah had his thoughts in order, he "contended with the nobles" (Neh. 5:7). He recognized that something had to be done, that he could not stand idly by while widows and children were enslaved and the property of the sick was seized by mortgage holders. So, *he communicated his carefully considered proposal*, insisting on action.

Your husband never puts his dirty shirt in the laundry basket? You can kick it, slam it into the basket, even tear it up in anger, but that will not change his habit. Notice that in Ephesians 4, before Paul's admonition on anger (v. 26) comes the command to speak the truth (v. 25). After Paul wrote, "let all bitterness and wrath and anger . . . be put away from you" (v. 31), he reminded us to "be kind to one another, tenderhearted" (v. 32). So instead of kicking the shirt every time it lies on the floor, talk to your husband about it at a time when you can do it kindly and dispassionately. Then if he should remind you of a habit that upsets him, you can also accept it without anger.

Nehemiah knew that if he kept quiet and stewed about the situation, a great deal of tension could build up. At the earliest opportunity he confronted the leadership and suggested a plan of action. No doubt it was tougher to do that than keep quiet, but the longer he waited, the harder it would get.

The devil has a way of helping us postpone positive, stress-reducing communication. Or he likes to see us skirt the issue, beat around the bush. Maybe we mention it in prayer meeting, asking others to pray about it, rather than taking the risk to move into a loving, biblical confrontation.

Or we simply avoid the topics that could provide disagreement. Maybe at this moment you are saying, "That's us. We never discuss discipline of our children" or "We never discuss my mother-in-law." Instead of resolving differences in loving communication, we let our bodies absorb the effects of that tension—and our children experience confusion because we as parents are not agreed on when and how to administer discipline; nor are they sure how to respond to the relatives.

When Nehemiah communicated his reaction to what he saw, he suggested a solution to the problem. He said, "Please, give back to them this very day" (Neh. 5:11)—and then he listed what needed to be restored. And it was done! Would that have happened if he had simply berated them in his anger?

Most solutions you and I propose will not get the response Nehemiah received. A compromise will be a more likely result. The husband working on the racing car with his friends may agree to a less frequent schedule and also to a greater involvement in the home. In return for watching a particular football game, the husband may agree to take his wife out to dinner at her favorite restaurant. *Whatever the compromise, the proposing of creative solutions is a far more effective release of energy than blowing up or clamming up.*

Are you married to one of those uncommunicative types, or do you work for one at the office or factory? There may be many times when the only thing you can do is to spend a lot of time communicating with God, asking for wisdom on how to unlock a life that does not want to communicate. You cannot simply give up, for if the person you are living with does not want to communicate, there are clearly unresolved conflicts he is not able to face. Guilt freezes the lines of communication.

Forgiveness may be the necessary alternative. In your anger, you may have been showing an unforgiving spirit that is blocking communication. The Bible is very clear that we are to forgive one another unconditionally, no matter how seriously we have been offended or hurt.

Sometimes repentance is the only solution. A father of five in Detroit went golfing early Sunday morning and then went to the church where a revival meeting was in progress. Of the 200 men attending the meeting, half were on their knees before God. When he saw the men weeping before God, he pounded his fist into his hand and said, "You'll never get me, God."

Why did he say that? Because he had a hot temper and five children, an unfortunate combination. Through the years he had deeply wounded the spirits of those children, and he knew that if God ever got hold of him, he would have to repent and ask forgiveness of his children. Eventually, God "got" him. When he sought the forgiveness of his children, the experience was used by the Lord to soften the hearts of the whole family.

Dealing with our anger may thus involve compromise, it may mean forgiving others who have wounded us and have not asked for forgiveness, and it may necessitate repentance. Only when this happens can the anger within us be resolved so it does not stay inside us forever.

Nehemiah represents the person who was good and angry. He was angry at sin and injustice, at the suffering of the poor at the hands of the greedy. He also represents the person who channels his anger creatively for positive results. He controlled his tongue until he had thought about the situation. Then he communicated in a positive manner what was in his heart. Finally, he proposed a solution that, though in many ways was unpalatable, could be implemented.

God does not want us to live with uncontrolled anger. He even sets a deadline—"Do not let the sun go down upon your anger" (Eph. 4:26). Only then will we avoid giving the devil an opportunity to lead us to sin. Then we will have the inner release that contributes to a healthy spirit, mind, and body. Ultimately that release is honoring to God, for it lets others know that the Holy

Spirit is in charge of our lives.

Application
If you have an uncontrollable temper, here are some specific instructions that will enable you to exercise control.

1. Choose to forgive those who have wronged you. Lay down all bitterness (Eph. 4:31).

2. Begin each day by resisting Satan, especially that spirit of anger, and focus your mind on the promises of God. (This must be done *before* you encounter those stressful situations during the day.

3. Accept your circumstances as coming from God. Your employer or partner is being used by God to develop the fruit of the Spirit in your life. Thank God for those difficult moments when you can prove His power.

4. Ask God to release the power of the Holy Spirit within you. Part of the fruit of the Spirit is "self-control."

5. If you *do* lose control, confess your sin to God and the person who was the object of your derision. Do this immediately.

6. Pray that God will give you wisdom to (a) become aware of a solution for the point of tension that causes the anger, and (b) communicate your feelings to the person involved in the right *way* and at the right *time*. Remember that your struggle is God's means of producing growth in your life.

9

Overcoming Disappointment

WHEN I joined the faculty of the Moody Bible Institute some years ago, the secretary for our section of faculty offices was a friendly, bright-eyed, 20-year-old woman whose cheerful smile greeted everyone who walked past her desk. Three months later, a massive tumor was found in her abdomen. The doctors concluded she had only three months to live.

Debbie left for a hospital that specialized in cancer treatment. When she came back, the cancer was in remission and it seemed as though she was cured. You can imagine the tremendous feelings of relief and joy in the family and among her new friends at Moody. But the cancer did start to grow again, and Debbie died some months later.

Can you visualize what it must have been like to be lifted to the heavens, as it were, with those great feelings of joy and anticipation for a new lease on life, only to have all hope dashed to the ground? During that time, Debbie no doubt had to fight a tremendous sense of disappointment, as did her family and friends. The temporary promise of healing only heightened the disappointment.

Yet people like Debbie are not the only ones experiencing deep feelings of disappointment. You take a new job in a new community, hoping to find a more congenial work environment, only to find that office politics are just as rampant as at the job you left. Your superior is promoted, and you know you can handle the job he left behind—but someone else gets it. He's 15 years younger than you are and not half as experienced.

As a parent, you may be disappointed in your children's actions. A woman who had once been a Bible class teacher said, "Long ago I'd given up on God and on prayer. For 19 years I prayed that my daughter would grow up to be a missionary. Not only has she not become a missionary, but she is now married to an unsaved man." Looking wistfully into the distance, she said, "I don't want to ask God for anything else because I don't want to be hurt and disappointed again."

Disappointment. It strikes all of us at one time or another. If these feelings are fed, they grow until they strangle our spiritual lives.

The Bible tells us about a time of severe disappointment experienced by the Children of Israel (Ex. 15:22-27). The Israelites had just come through the Red Sea, which the Lord had gloriously opened up for them. The first part of Exodus 15 records their response to what God had done. It is a song so full of ecstatic praise that you are sure they will trust the Lord even in the most difficult of situations. (Eons later, another triumphant group will also sing "the song of Moses," as described in Revelation 15:3. These will also have "come off victorious from the beast and from his image and from the number of his name, standing on the sea of glass, holding harps of God" [Rev. 15:2]. Their song will be: "Great and marvelous are Thy works, O Lord God, the Almighty" [v.3]).

But the heights of ecstasy did not last long in Moses' day! Tramping across the hot desert sand quickly reduced the Israelites' supply of water to a sip now and then. For three days they looked for water and found none. Repeatedly the scouts came back with negative reports. It is clear from the tone of the narrative that anxiety was increasing.

Let me assure you before continuing that this is not just a story of the Israelites. It is our story as well. To recognize that, we must understand their circumstances better.

Some years ago I was at Mount Sinai. We spent two days in a bus going from Jerusalem to Mount Sinai, and two days in our return. I vividly remember those buses getting stuck in the sand. We had to get out and push our bus just as though we were stuck in a snowbank. I remember how thirsty we became. We determined, however, not to drink any water except what we had brought along, fearing we would get sick if we drank any other. But when our water ran out, we drank whatever water was available.

"But surely Israel could have trusted God," you say. Yet for the Children of Israel in the desert, God seemed to be as elusive as the water they were looking for. Remember, this was at the start of 40 years of maturing in the faith, and they had a long way to grow before they could be called spiritually strong.

Then came the word, "We have found an oasis There's water just ahead." Parents encouraged their children, saying, "Just one more mile and we'll be there." Yet when they arrived, they discovered water so bitter they could not drink it.

"They were not thirsty enough," you say. Not true, for there are places where the water is so bitter that you cannot swallow it even if you are burning with thirst.

Then the grumbling set in. They had experienced a tremendous feeling of exhilaration as they approached the oasis, convinced that they would be able to slake their thirst. This made the disappointment so much greater—how could God play games with them? He led them to an oasis and their hopes soared, only to be dashed to the ground.

Disappointment Is a Test

We can learn some lessons about overcoming disappointment from this experience of the Children of Israel. We will ask several questions. First, what causes disappointment?

The answer is a wrong focus. The Children of Israel had their minds and hearts set on two things. The first was the desire for water. I am not blaming them, for I am quite sure I would have been looking at the same thing. Yet the Israelites had their hearts so set on water, and on drinking it, that when the seemingly improved circumstances proved unsatisfactory, they blamed Moses and God.

They did not remember, as we don't most of the time, that when our hearts are set on something in this world, we stand a good chance of experiencing bitter disappointment. You have set your heart, for example, on getting a promotion. As far as you are concerned, it is "in the bag." Done. You have worked hard for it and you deserve it. When it is given to another, the bottom drops out of your world.

Or maybe you had your heart set on marriage. You meet another person with the same desire. You sense that it will work. Yet soon after the wedding, you realize he's not the kind of husband you expected. As the years pass, the differences grow, as does the strain in the marriage relationship. Initially the disappointment is mingled with the hope that things will get better. As the days roll into months and years, there is less hope and more disappointment. Why did God let this happen to you?

In both instances, as in Israel, the focus was on the circumstances, not on God. You were hoping circumstances would bring you joy, forgetting that joy comes only out of your relationship with Jesus Christ. As long as our hope is based on some thing or a combination of circumstances in this world, the risk of disappointment is great.

Second, the Children of Israel had their hopes pinned on a person, Moses. After all, he had been involved in such an astonishing number of miracles. So when the water was bitter, they grumbled to Moses, "So what's this? You take us into the desert three days and lead us to an oasis with bitter water. What kind of leadership is that?"

You know, of course, that they were not really grumbling against Moses. Their complaint was with God. Every complaint against the circumstances of life, unless they can be changed by us, is in reality a complaint against God. When it is cold and the snow is piled 10 feet high, we complain about it. Then when summer comes and the heat and humidity wilt collars and raise tempers, we complain again. Since God is in control of the weather, our complaints are really aimed at Him.

On a list of 10 reasons why marriages fail, unrealistic expectations is at the top. People expect a partner to provide what only God can do for them. One woman wrote that she had made her "Prince Charming" the king in her life. When he left her after 20 years of marriage, she was no longer the queen, and it devastated her. She made little progress, despite several stays in a mental hospital, until a friend invited her to a Bible study. There she found that Jesus could meet her heart's needs in a way her husband had never been able to.

You say, "I am happily married and that would never happen to me." But any human being is a potential broken reed. Only Jesus will never disappoint you. For that reason alone, your focus, even in a happy marriage, needs to be on your relationship with God.

One of the most widespread causes for disappointment is the discovery that a spiritual leader has feet of clay. We can put up with bad breath, with his not always remembering names. But when he loses his temper, when he is rude to a waitress, or if he fails morally, we can be shaken in our faith in God because the disappointment is so great. Unfortunately, we have superstars in Christianity just as the world has its superstars. We forget that Jesus alone is the "superstar" in Christianity. The psalmist had come to terms with that when he wrote, "My soul, wait in silence for God only, for my hope is from Him" (Ps. 62:5). That's an important lesson to learn if we want to overcome life's disappointments.

Have you ever thought that our disappointments are God's way of reminding us that there are idols in our lives that must be dealt with? In Psalm 73, the Psalmist Asaph told us that he looked at the rich and noticed that they were often wicked people. He wondered why he did not have wealth like that as a servant of God. He admitted, "My steps had almost slipped. For I was envious of the arrogant, as I saw the prosperity of the wicked" (73:2-3). Then one day he went into the temple and God reminded him of the end of the wicked. He quickly realized that the rich were indeed in deep trouble and that his riches were in reality far greater than theirs. That's why he could say, "Whom have I in heaven but Thee? And besides Thee, I desire nothing on earth" (v. 25). In effect he said, "God, You are my all." It is only when you discover that you have nothing left but God that you realize God is enough.

The Children of Israel arrived at Marah, their hearts set on improved circumstances, on an abundance of sweet water, on another great display of leadership by Moses, and they were severely disappointed. They had not yet learned that God wants us to recognize that He alone is the One who can fully meet our expectations.

I remember how I had to learn this lesson. I was extremely elated by the response of someone I greatly admired to something I had written. As I was rejoicing, the

Holy Spirit put a damper on my joy, reminding me that some things I would do would be severely criticized. If my heart was set on getting the praise of men, I would sooner or later be disappointed. But if I looked for God's approval, He would not disappoint me.

Disappointment Is an Opportunity

What is the remedy for disappointment? Moses had listened to the grumbling of the people. You can take only so much of that, so he shut them out and started talking to God. In fact, the Bible uses a much stronger word than that: he cried out to the Lord. The Lord responded by showing him a tree that he cut down and threw into the water. Whether the tree was known for its ability to turn bitter water into sweet drinking water does not matter. The fact is that Moses saw the tree only when he called upon the Lord.

When Hurricane Allen hit the coast of Texas, it carried a tidal wave in front of it. Right about now you may feel as though you have been hit by that tidal wave, your disappointment is so great. All you can think about is unrealized expectations. Yet now is the time to remember what Moses did—he cried out to the Lord.

Prayer is that mighty power that is swifter than an eagle, stronger than a lion. Prayer puts you in touch with the resources of a compassionate and holy God. And when Moses prayed, a miracle started unfolding. He saw a tree that turned their situation totally around, that alleviated their disappointment.

Even if the tree had the ability to turn bitter water into sweet water, there's no way it could have been effective for all the water on the oasis. God did a miracle, changing the bitter water into the sweetest drinking water Israel had ever known. That's one way God responds to our disappointments. He changes the circumstances in response to prayer.

There are times when life's disappointments become

God's opportunity to do a miracle. The person who was promoted ahead of you is hired away by another company, and this time you get promoted. Your marriage partner goes off to a retreat, meets the Lord in a vital way, and begins fulfilling your expectations. Your child joins a canoeing expedition and there in the wilderness recognizes the rotten way he's been treating you.

Remember when Jesus calmed the sea with but a word? (Matt. 8:26) Remember how the storm stopped when Jesus got into the boat after He came walking to the disciples on the water? (14:25-32) He changed the water into wine (John 2:1-10), raised Jairus' daughter (Matt. 9:24-25) and the son of the widow of Nain (Luke 7:13-15), and fed 5,000 with five loaves and two fish (9:16-17). He can do it today.

I believe, however, that God wants to do an even greater miracle than turning our bitter circumstances into something sweet. Suppose you have a very responsible position in your community. You are determined that nothing, no one, not even your children, will damage your reputation. Then your son goes to a party where there are alcoholic beverages, and he gets drunk. On the way home, he loses control of his car and it crashes into a tree. The girl with him is killed, and your son walks away almost unscathed. Not surprisingly, you and your wife are very angry, bitter about a home that served alcohol, and resentful that your son is now the talk of the town.

What would be the greatest miracle in relation to your disappointment? Would it not be taking away the resentment and bitterness, the anger and extreme disappointment, replacing it with the grace and ability to accept that son even though he disappointed you? God can do it and is doing it in families today.

God can begin to make you accept that person your daughter married. He can give you inner release from the anger generated when your husband is trapped by his desires on a business trip. The circumstances may remain unchanged, but God can help you to discover His sweetness in the midst of bitter water.

Furthermore, many people believe that the tree Moses threw into the bitter water was symbolic of the Cross. You'll remember that Eve ate from the forbidden tree and then gave the fruit to Adam, who also ate. That tree poisoned all the waters of humanity from that time on. The Gospels draw our attention to another tree, the Cross on which Jesus Christ died, absorbing all the hurts and disappointments, all the consequences of sin, for all humanity. He thereby made a payment for sin so that man could be in touch with God again, providing a way through which the bitterness of life could become sweet. Even death, the most bitter of experiences, can be sweetened because of the Cross.

The Apostle Paul reminded us of the significance of the Cross in Galatians 6:14. Though he had experienced many bitter disappointments in life, he wrote, "But may it never be that I should boast, except in the Cross of our Lord Jesus Christ." *He knew that if you begin to glory in something other than the Cross, you are headed for disappointment.* It may be at the beginning of life, in the middle of life, or at the end, but the disappointment will come.

Notice Paul's conclusion: "Through which the world has been crucified to me, and I to the world" (v. 14). He was saying that God takes care of life's disappointments by weaning us from all the world's secret pleasures, making us dead to all those impulses that are not honoring to the Lord. As we, through the Holy Spirit, come alive to God, He can somehow sweeten life's harsh and bitter experiences.

That does not mean we become immune to all the disappointments of life. Disappointments will come because we remain human. But it does mean that those bitter waters of disappointment can be made sweet through the forgiveness of Christ and the acceptance we receive in Christ through the power of the Cross.

Think of that disappointment that is eating away at you right now. Bring it to the Cross, receive forgiveness for your lack of faith and trust in God, and expose it to His ability to heal.

Disappointment Can Be a Stepping-Stone

What is the challenge of disappointment? As I see it, the challenge is to obedience. Notice Exodus 15:25-26: "There He made for them a statute and regulation, and there He tested them. And He said, 'If you will give earnest heed to the voice of the Lord your God, and do what is right in His sight, and give ear to His commandments, and keep all His statutes, I will put none of the diseases on you which I have put on the Egyptians; for I, the Lord, am your healer.'"

According to the biblical record, the experience at Marah was a test, establishing a pattern that God followed throughout the Old Testament. God *tested* the Children of Israel to see what was in their hearts, to see if they would really keep His commandments.

Focus on that disappointment in your life. Think of it in terms of a test permitted by God to see if you will obey Him, trust Him, believe that He desires the best for you. Or are you going to say, "OK, God, it's all over. I'm through. I'm finished with You. You did not take care of this circumstance as I expected You would. You didn't answer my prayer. You didn't do what I *knew* You ought to do, so I'm through."

If you think of every disappointment as a test, it becomes an opportunity to say, "God, I'm going to readjust my focus. I'm going to learn my lesson. I'm going to trust You to do that miracle in my heart."

After the test of obedience, the Children of Israel experienced God's reward. He had told them that if they responded properly, He would not afflict them with all the diseases He had put on the Egyptians during the plagues. In effect, the Lord said, "I will be in the midst of your circumstances. I will protect you from some of the harsh realities of existence. I will bring you all the way into the land because I will physically give you the strength, and I will protect you from disease."

Immediately after this commitment on God's part, the people arrived at Elim, where there were 12 springs, one for every tribe in Israel. Seventy date palms dotted the skyline to relieve the monotony of the desert, and it may be that they also provided a change in diet. Supplied with all the water they needed, the Children of Israel settled down for a refreshing interlude.

Have you ever noticed that disappointments give life a roller-coaster effect? You go through extremely disappointing times, not realizing there is an Elim ahead. Even the tall palms are not yet visible. Yet God has a reward waiting when you pass the test of obedience, something extra-special if you obey His voice.

Several years ago I met a young man in Denver who is very good at speculating on where oil wells might be. Not surprisingly, he has become very wealthy. One time he made a bid on a contract that was very important to him. Because of a technicality, he missed getting the contract. He told me that when he came home, he felt so disappointed that he became physically sick. In telling me about it he said, "As a result of that experience, I made a vow to God that I would never again set my heart on anything in this world other than my relationship to the Lord God." That young man responded correctly to the test of obedience. Subsequently, he was awarded contracts many times larger than the one he failed to win.

I've met many people who have had bitterly disappointing experiences. I've discovered that a variety of "trees" has been offered to them. You may even have tried to sweeten the bitter water in your life with one of them.

One of the trees highly recommended to remove bitterness is riches. People think that if they could only become rich, all the bitterness would disappear. Yet there is ample evidence in the personal testimony of rich people that riches are no cure for disappointments. In fact, they turn bitter water into poison.

Another highly recommended tree is the tree of pleasure. It grows with sturdy and deep roots. It promises to remove the monotony of existence and replace it with excitement and glitter. Just nibble at it, people say, and you'll find it a lot easier to make it from weekend to weekend. Yet even though man has more time for pleasure and a greater variety of ways to experience it, we see unhappiness everywhere. The divorce rate is just one indication that people are not happier.

For years, drugs and alcohol were promoted as the great escape from disappointment. But the increasing rate of suicide among people who use drugs and alcohol clearly shows that this tree cannot sweeten the bitter waters.

The greatest disappointments in life come from unfulfilled expectations, unrealized dreams, and the only "tree" that will sweeten the bitter waters of disappointment is the Lord Himself. The Apostle Paul came to realize this after he met Christ. He wrote, "I count all things to be loss in view of the surpassing value of knowing Christ Jesus my Lord, for whom I have suffered the loss of all things, and count them but rubbish in order that I may gain Christ" (Phil. 3:8).

Only when your expectations are focused on Christ can you overcome the disappointments of life. He is an expert at healing the brokenhearted. Thus, your *disappointment* can become God's *appointment* to discover that He alone must be your pleasure, your desire, the focus of your heart's affection.

Application

1. Study Luke 24:1-35 as an example of the cause and cure for disappointment. Answer these questions:

● Since the disciples' concept of the Messiah was quite accurate (vv. 19-21), what specifically caused them to be so disappointed in Him?

● What very important bits of information were the disciples missing in their concept of what they expected Christ to do or not to do?

● To what did Christ point them in their disappointment, and how should it have helped them?

● These disciples eventually returned to Jerusalem with courage and joy. What made the difference? How should this apply to us today?

2. Give examples of disappointments in your own life. Were your hopes pinned on some circumstances or human goal? What lesson, if any, did you learn from these experiences?

10

Moving from Regret to Restoration

"FOR of all the sad words of tongue and pen, the saddest are these, 'It might have been.'" So wrote John Greenleaf Whittier.

I think all of us can identify with that statement. All of us have suffered from feelings of regret. We know the pain and agony regret brings into our lives. We keep thinking how really different it all could have been if—if—if. You complete the sentence.

There are at least two kinds of regret. There is the regret caused by making human error. You make an honest mistake, but it may have had disastrous consequences, and you have to live with them.

I read of an incident involving a missionary airplane mechanic. He had serviced airplanes for years and had an excellent record. One day he had just completed the initial hand-tightening on a nut when he was called away. Completely distracted by the new problem, he forgot to tighten the nut with a wrench.

The airplane took off with seven people in it. Because that nut was not adequately tightened, gasoline started leaking out. The plane eventually caught fire and crashed, killing all seven aboard.

That mechanic attended the funeral and saw the seven coffins lined up in a row. Waves of regret washed over him in his agony of soul and spirit. One momentary lapse and seven lives had been snuffed out. Children lost their fathers, and there were several mothers widowed.

You may have been driving carefully in a residential district. The curb was lined with cars. You were distracted by a person on one side of the street for a moment. As your eyes refocused on the road ahead of you, you saw a toddler run into the street. You slammed on the brakes, but it was too late. As a result, you experience tremendous feelings of regret.

In such cases, we must ask others to forgive us for our errors in judgment. The missionary mechanic was fortunate because he was assured by the bereaved that they understood that everyone makes errors. They were not angry at him. It took months, but eventually the mechanic overcame his despondency and fierce regret. Receiving the forgiveness of others enabled him to forgive himself.

Though such feelings of regret are difficult to live with, they are not brought on by the Holy Spirit. They result from human error, which we are all subject to daily. Some of us are more prone to such error because of lack of education, experience, or physical limitations. However, it is not God's intention that we get bogged down by our inability to forgive ourselves. Our mistakes must be put behind us.

There's a second form of regret that grows out of deliberate disobedience. We choose a certain lifestyle even though we know it is wrong. A small voice in us tells us our choice is sinful, but we continue in that lifestyle anyway. One day we look in the family album and see what we looked like as a little boy or little girl, and we suddenly wonder what life would have been like if our choices had been different.

Or the regret may come at the end of life as death

approaches. A friend went to see a former employer, a newspaper publisher, in the hospital. When the publisher saw my friend, he asked that the door be closed. Then he asked that my friend read the Bible for him and pray with him.

"I know I am going to die. I have wasted my life in a vain pursuit of riches and public acclaim. Now I realize my mistake and want to get right with God," the publisher said.

Sometimes a father experiences a similar regret when his children have all left home. He wishes he had taken more time with them—he hardly knows them now. The regret will not change what has happened in the past, but it can lead to future changes. God can still use that emotion of regret to make the best of the future.

How Could I Have Done That?
So what can you do about regret? What response will minimize the agony of regret and help you cope with the memory of missed opportunities or wrong decisions? The Bible provides an example that can be most helpful to you and me.

The initial incident is found in Luke 22:31-34. Read it carefully, for it sets the stage for a decision that Peter, the disciple of Christ, will deeply regret.

Peter is at the final meal with Jesus. They have just had what we now call the Lord's Supper. Then the disciples got into a major argument over who was the greatest among them, a development Jesus used to teach them about servant-leadership roles. I sense that Peter must have been a central figure in the argument, for Jesus turned to him by name and warned him that Satan desired to sift him like wheat. Then Jesus said something that came back to haunt Peter: "I have prayed for you, that your faith may not fail; and you, when once you have turned again, strengthen your brothers" (v. 32). The implication is that Peter would fail and be restored.

Peter did not like that implication. He had all the credentials for being a winning member of the team, so he decided to reassure Jesus. He proudly asserted, "Lord, with You I am ready to go both to prison and to death!" (v. 33)

Have you ever prayed and thought to yourself, *God ought to be really impressed with the promise I am making. At least He can depend on me.* As you thought that, you had forgotten that you can keep no promises made to God except the ones made in total dependence upon Him, recognizing the need for His grace to live as you should.

Weeks and months later, Peter may have been saying to himself, *Me and my big mouth. I'm constantly getting in deeper than I can handle. If only I didn't need to show off my commitment so much.* You see, the bigger the promise, the harder the fall.

You know the rest of the story. Peter obviously boasted too much, prayed too little, acted too soon, and almost got himself arrested for cutting off a guard's ear. Later he followed too far off, considered what he was saying too little, and generally ended up digging a real grave for himself. The crow of a rooster and a glance from Jesus brought him down to earth. Mark, the Gospel writer, reported the result: "And he began to weep" (Mark 14:72).

Why did Peter weep bitterly? I think it was because he was in the very presence of Jesus when he denied Him. Jesus was within the line of his vision when the servant girl came and said to him, "You, too, were with Jesus the Nazarene" (v. 67). Overcome by fear of the results if he admitted allegiance to his Master, Peter denied that he had ever known Jesus (v. 68).

Those kinds of denials are hard to understand and accept. Peter had been with Jesus three years. He had shared the platform with Him at many large gatherings. Jesus had healed his mother-in-law. And Peter had made that soul-stirring affirmation, "Thou art the Christ, the

Son of the living God" (Matt. 16:16). Now the accusing tone in a girl's voice brought from Peter's lips an abject denial. In fact, I suspect Peter later had trouble accepting the fact that he had really done it. He couldn't believe his own memory. That's regret.

In spite of all that, Peter's experience provides us with clear guidelines on how to move from regret to restoration; how you can move from bitterness over some experience in your past to blessing. Through the experience of Peter, God draws back the curtain a bit and lets us gain at least some understanding of what is going on in the great drama of life. It shows how you who are living in the far country of regret can be restored to meaningful fellowship with the Saviour.

Christ Intercedes for Us

The first truth to accept is that *Jesus Christ prays for you*. When you examine Luke 22:31, you will notice that Jesus addressed Peter as "Simon," using the name that refers to his humanity. At that moment he was not Peter, the rock, but Simon, the human being, open to the temptation of Satan.

There is an interesting contrast in the Greek New Testament. When Jesus said, "Satan has demanded permission to sift you," the word *you* is plural. Christ was apparently speaking to all the disciples. But when He continued, "But I have prayed for you" (v. 32), the word *you* is singular. Now the focus is directly on Peter, that his faith won't fail.

Why did Jesus pray for Peter? Was it because Peter held such a lofty position in the group? Hardly. Peter was the rash and egotistical one. He was not the mild-mannered, consistent follower.

"Aha," you say. "I know why Jesus prayed for Peter. It was because Peter was the bold, strong one, the man who was able to make wise decisions for the group."

Wrong again. The reason Jesus prayed for Peter was

precisely that he was so weak, that he was the kind of person who could be tripped up easily. You show me a man who is wretched, who is broken up emotionally, who cries out to God in the agony of his soul; you show me a woman who is fallen and crushed by her sin, who is unstable and unable to get a grip on her emotions; and I will show you a person upon whom the grace and mercy of Jesus Christ rest.

You remember the story of the shepherd. He had 99 fine, obedient sheep in the fold. Yet there was one that had gone astray, who was outside in the night, and that is the one who got the attention of the shepherd (Luke 15:4-6). In the same way, Jesus sees everyone reading this page, but He is looking particularly at the one who is following afar off, whose faith has almost failed, who has denied the Lord and seems to be outside the embrace of God. He has prayed for you in a personal way, as He prayed especially for Peter so that he would not be totally overwhelmed by regret.

Significantly, Jesus' prayer is not a "bless everyone" generalization. It has a focus—Satan and his activity in the life of Peter. Jesus said, "Simon, Simon, behold, Satan has demanded permission to sift you like wheat; but I have prayed for you, that your faith may not fail" (vv. 31-32).

When wheat grows, it has a protective coating called chaff around the grain. In the old-fashioned winnowing of Jesus' day, the chaff was separated from the wheat by throwing the mixture into the air while the wind was blowing. Modern harvesting equipment uses a sieve. Jesus was saying to Peter, "Satan wants to sift you and prove that you are nothing but chaff."

You ask, "Does my exposure to temptation really have anything to do with evil spirits? Does it have anything to do with Satan?" Yes, it does. Peter did not see it that way, nor do many people today. But the Lord opens the curtain so that we can see behind the scene and know that there are evil spirits who want to deflect us from our commitments to Jesus Christ.

Every Christian goes through this sifting process, not just those who experience some of the more obvious trials such as illness, loss of a job, or persecution on the job or in the classroom. If you have ever been tempted, and all of us have, you should know that Satan not only desires to have you, but he has already made meticulous plans for your downfall. It is as though he were sitting there, coiled up and ready to spring up and get you to fall so that all who are watching will think there is little substance to your commitment to Jesus Christ.

So today, as He did to Peter, Jesus is saying, "Satan has asked permission, and it has been granted, just as in the case of Job, to test you. When the temptation is over, I pray that your faith will not fail. And when you have turned back, strengthen your brethren. When you fail, do not let the regret over your failure destroy you and your witness, but remember that I have prayed for you." Right now, Jesus is before God as your High Priest and remembers you to the Father.

Christ Understands Us

The fact that Jesus has prayed for us and is interceding for us right now is great news when we are experiencing regret. There is, however, more good news—*Jesus knows exactly who we are.*

Remember when Jesus said to Peter, "The cock will not crow today until you have denied three times that you know Me"? (Luke 22:34) Did He say that merely to prove His omniscience? No, the significance to Peter and to us goes far beyond that. The statement revealed that Jesus knew both the circumstances Peter would get into and Peter's weakness.

Consider what Jesus said. He clearly identified the circumstances in which Peter would deny Him. I am convinced He knew precisely where Peter would be seated.

He knew that the servant girl would come along and accuse Peter of belonging to Jesus. Incredibly, He knew there would be a rooster in the area who would crow just at the right time to alert Peter to his sin. The Bible report reveals that while Peter was still speaking, the rooster began crowing—perfect timing.

God knows the circumstances that led to your temptation, to your sin, to your failure as a human being. He has accurate knowledge of every temptation, every struggle, and every dilemma that you will encounter. That is why He can deal with your regret as well.

Jesus knew Peter's weakness, and He knows your weakness. In effect, He said to Peter, "Peter, when you get the chance to say yes to Me and testify for Me, you are going to say no. You are going to be scared to death to identify yourself with Me. Even though outwardly you have often put on a good show, I know how weak you are inside."

Why did Jesus tell Peter that? He wanted to make it easy for Peter to come back to Him. He wanted Peter to know that the hidden weakness revealed during the temptation was no surprise to Him. And He wants us to know it.

A student came to me one day and said, "Oh, I can't face God about this sin again. I can't even face God about my weakness." She thought that possibly God would be shocked. I suggested that He would be disappointed, but He is never caught off guard by our weaknesses. In fact, Jesus knows things about you that you have not even admitted to yourself. You would not want to know the potential for wickedness in your heart, but God knows. That is why He is able to help you cope with regret.

Christ Has Compassion for Us

We have established that you can cope with regret because Jesus prayed for you and Jesus knows your circumstances and weaknesses. There is a third facet of Peter's experience that is of great value when you are weighed down with regret. *Jesus had compassion for Peter, and He has the same compassion for you.*

If you have experienced any depth of regret, you will have some idea of the torture Peter must have gone through for the three days after the crucifixion of Jesus. Round and round in his head whirled thoughts like, *My last chance to prove my loyalty. My opportunity to confirm my allegiance, and I deny Him. Not once, not twice, but three times! Lord, why did I do it? I'll never be able to forgive myself as long as I live.*

If someone had asked Peter during that time, "Are you a disciple of Jesus?" he may very well have said, "I was one, but I am no longer worthy of that high honor. I've struck out, and I know I'm not going to be included in any future accounting of the 12 disciples of Jesus. His book on me is closed."

Yet that is not the way Jesus treated Peter. Take a look at Mark 16:7. Jesus, speaking to the women who had come to the tomb, said, "But go, tell His disciples *and Peter*" (author's italics added). Just put yourself in the place of those women and imagine what was going on in their minds at that moment. I suspect they were so overwhelmed by the reality of Jesus' resurrection that the final phrase, "and Peter," didn't register too clearly. If it did, they must have wondered about the great compassion of Jesus, clearly forgiving the one who had denied Him three times. That compassion is, however, totally typical of Jesus

I trust the women gave Peter Jesus' message. Even if they did not, Jesus' compassion is demonstrated by another phrase in the Gospel of Luke. In chapter 24, we read the story of the two disciples who were walking to Emmaus when they were joined by Jesus. After Luke described the whole dramatic incident, he recorded their return to Jerusalem, where they were told, "The Lord has really risen, and has appeared to Simon" (v. 34). In 1 Corinthians 15, the Apostle Paul listed the appearances of Jesus after His resurrection, putting the appearance to Peter (Cephas) at the head of the list, indicating Peter was the first to see Jesus (v. 5). That incident clearly demonstrated that Peter did not need to live with regret any longer. A compassionate Jesus had forgiven him.

Imagine the scene. Jesus puts His arms around Peter, looks in his eyes, and says, "Peter, you fell, but you are not down. You have denied Me, but I am not finished with you yet. You have sinned, but you wept tears of repentance and you are forgiven. I love you, Peter."

The arms of Jesus even now are reaching out to you in your regret. They are long enough and gentle enough to embrace even the most wayward, backslidden person who has denied the Saviour. Jesus has His eyes fastened on you, and He says, "I have compassion on you. I will go out of My way to assure you that you can come back into fellowship with the living God."

Christ Restores Us

There is a fourth essential truth if we are to deal effectively with regret, and this is illustrated in John 21:15-17. It is the last stage in the restoration of Peter. In one of the most tender scenes in the Bible, Jesus asked Peter, "Simon, son of John, do you love Me more than these?" (v. 15) Peter responded with a different word for love, brotherly love, instead of the self-giving, agape love Jesus asked about. Jesus then showed He understood by saying, "Tend My lambs" (v. 15). "OK," Jesus was saying, "You may not feel ready for heavy-duty action yet, but you can start by looking after the lambs in God's flock."

The ever-present Jesus then repeated the question, again asking if Peter had that true agape love for Him. Peter was not yet sure of his own heart, so he responded, "Yes, I love You, but with a brotherly love." Jesus replied, "Shepherd My sheep" (v. 16). In effect He said, "I know where you are coming from, but I am sure you can handle more than the lambs."

I don't know how much time elapsed, but a third time Jesus asked, "Do you love me with a phileo (brotherly) love?" Peter was grieved, disturbed that his commitment of brotherly love was not enough, but he repeated his affirmation of love for the third time. Jesus accepted it and said, "Tend My sheep" (v. 17). In effect He said, "I know you are not sure of yourself yet, but I know I can trust you to be a shepherd to God's sheep. Don't let your regret hold you back from the high calling I have given you."

With these new responsibilities, Jesus had restored Peter to his former position of leadership. Regret was replaced by responsibility, indicating full acceptance. Three denials were followed by three affirmations of love and a growing responsibility.

Let's go back to Jesus' prayer for Peter. Just because Jesus prayed for Peter did not mean that Peter could not fail. Christ's prayer did not prevent Peter from launching into an impassioned denial of Jesus Christ. But Jesus had said that He was praying for Peter so that "your faith will not fail" in spite of the sin. "Peter," Jesus was saying, "when you have repented and have come back into fellowship with Me, then you can go ahead and feed My sheep."

You would not expect much strength from someone like Peter, would you? Yet sometimes those who have fallen the most, who have been the most overt in their denial of Christ, are the most effective in strengthening the feet of those who have fallen. Think of Peter preaching that great sermon on Pentecost. Read the fantastic encouragement in both 1 and 2 Peter as proof of that.

We have drawn our lessons from only one person who was sifted by Satan during the time preceding the Crucifixion. Yet there were two others. One was Christ Himself, sifted by Satan as He prayed in the Garden of Gethsemane. Many think Satan actually tried to kill Jesus there because of the great agony of spirit that He experienced. Yet Jesus turned out to be pure wheat.

Judas was the other person sifted by Satan. Remember how he kissed Jesus on the cheek? Yet he denied the Lord for the sake of money. Judas was so filled with remorse that he went and hanged himself. He was sifted by Satan and revealed to be pure chaff.

Peter, like most of us, turned out to be part chaff and part wheat. The process of sifting was one of God's ways of separating the chaff from the wheat. As Peter saw his helplessness and learned to depend on the Holy Spirit, he became a completely different person.

Outwardly, Peter and Judas did essentially the same thing. Both were then filled with regret. Judas, instead of responding to the Saviour, let the regret and remorse overwhelm him. He is like many people who, because of financial reverses, because of personal problems in the family, or because they failed themselves and their families, close the ledger by taking their own lives. They live in hell with that regret, for it is regret that helps to make hell truly hell.

Peter, on the other hand, responded to the look of the Saviour. He moved closer to the Master through regret instead of away from Him. If you let the Holy Spirit do that while you are experiencing intense regret, He will restore you whether you are in your teens, 20s, 30s, or even 90s. Jesus Christ will then recommission you and say "OK, now strengthen others."

How do you move from regret to restoration? Accept the fact that Jesus has prayed for you and is now praying for you. Remember that He knows you through and through—and every circumstance you are in. Let His compassion flow out to you and embrace you in forgiving love as you honestly repent of what you have done. Relax in His total acceptance of you, no matter what happened to you or how you sinned. Finally, know that He has restored you to fellowship and new responsibilities. You'll be surprised at how beautifully God will direct you in the future if you let Him forgive the regrets of the past.

Application

1. List the experiences, the words, and the actions you have taken that still arouse feelings of regret. If they come to mind readily, they are still clearly troublesome.

2. Examine some of the Bible's examples of actions and words that must have brought on feelings of regret. Examples: Reuben (Gen. 37 and 45, particularly 45: 5-8); David (2 Sam. 11, compared with Ps. 51; also 2 Sam. 24).

3. What are the three steps in each example?

4. What can we learn from Psalm 32 about handling the regret that comes with sin?

5. What is the catalog of activity that caused Paul regret? (1 Tim. 1:13) How could he overcome the regret he felt? (vv. 13-16)

6. Now consider the answers you gave in number 1 in the light of David's prayers in Psalms 32 and 51 and Paul's statements in 1 Timothy 1:13-16.

11

Tackling the Bitter, Unforgiving Feeling

OUTSIDE, the autumn leaves spilled color across the rolling countryside. Inside, the mood was anything but bright as Karen settled into the pillows for a sleep-inducing chapter of her book. A quick glance at the chapter heading only increased the gloom. The last thing she wanted to read about was "Forgive Us Our Sins . . . As We Forgive Those Who Sin Against Us." She flung the book across the room.

She had every right to be bitter and unforgiving, she told herself as she lay awake that night. Her best friend from junior high days had refused all social contacts with her for the past two years. Though Karen had repeatedly tried to bridge the gap, her friend had maintained her distance. Annoyance had grown into resentment, and resentment into anger. Yes, of course Karen was bitter, but didn't she have a right to be?

Karen's feelings are all too common, even among Christians. There is Bill, who feels that his boss is out to make life miserable for him. He seems to criticize everything Bill does and demeans him in front of the other employees. After three years of this treatment, Bill is ready to explode, and a few days later, he does!

Doris knows all about feelings of anger and bitterness developing into a hard, unforgiving spirit. She was physically abused by a weak father who beat his children because of his anger at the world. Her mother retreated to hidden caches of wine, leaving Doris in charge of cleaning the house and doing the laundry by the time she was 10. Even though her parents are both dead, she has not yet forgiven them.

Perhaps the most excruciating experience of bitterness I know is the case of a husband who left town with his two small children, never to be seen again. His wife was left utterly alone in her anguish, fearful that she would never see her children again. Who can comprehend her anguish? Who would not understand if she began carrying a heavy load of bitterness toward her unfeeling husband?

Every one of us has known such feelings of hurt, anger, and bitterness at one time or another. We knew we ought to forgive, but either we could not get ourselves to do it or we did not want to. Nursing feelings of bitterness can be very satisfying as a form of revenge.

Being a Christian, or even having a position of leadership in the church, does not exempt us. For example, consider the disciples of Christ. Did they have the kinds of differences that led to resentment and anger? Yes, they did, for even after being with the Lord Jesus Christ for more than three years, they were still arguing over who would be the greatest in the kingdom.

I can imagine that Matthew was bothered by Peter because he talked too much. James may have resented his brother John, for John makes it quite clear that he was the disciple Jesus loved. In fact, there may have been others who resented this obvious favorite of Jesus. Or think of Philip, who may well have been embarrassed by Andrew's habit of talking about Jesus to everyone he met. He was forever missing the bus to the next meeting because he was tied up with someone! The disciples were human, and they undoubtedly had disagreements as they lived together as disciples of Christ. Struggles for position, tensions over priorities (such as when the children came to Jesus with their mothers), and personality conflicts are reported in the Bible. Jesus was aware of these. In fact, it is clear that some of His teachings dealt with those feelings of His followers.

The Goal of Forgiveness

When considering the importance of forgiveness, most of us turn to Matthew 18:21. Yet the opening word, "Then," indicates that Peter's question, "Lord, how often shall my brother sin against me and I forgive him?" was triggered by the previous discussion. Notice verse 15: "And if your brother sins, go and reprove him in private; if he listens to you, you have won your brother." The following verses expand on this theme, revealing the pattern for restoring an erring brother or sister. In verse 21, Peter seems to have wondered out loud what to do when a brother refused to be restored despite the loving encouragement of other Christians. He appears not to have noticed that Jesus' focus was not on the one sinned against, but on the sinning one.

When the Holy Spirit approaches us about our need to forgive someone who has sinned against us, we are usually more concerned about our feelings. We tend to focus on *our* need to forgive, on overcoming *our* bitterness and anger. The whole exercise and experience of forgiving someone else is designed, we are convinced, solely to help us feel better.

But by implication, Jesus, in Matthew 18:15 taught that focusing on our feelings is wrong. The goal is not to get us straightened out; it is to restore the brother or sister to fellowship We are not to be as concerned about our clear consciences as we are about the restoration into fellowship of the person who has sinned against us In other words, the goal of forgiveness is restoration.

⌄When we become truly concerned about the broken relationships with our brothers or sisters, we will become more concerned about them than we are about ourselves. When that happens, the anger and bitterness and the unforgiving spirit are naturally dissolved in our concern for the other person. This is particularly true when we do exactly what Jesus tells us to do: "Go and reprove him in private" (v. 15). There is no way you can maintain your anger, bitterness, and unforgiving spirit as you meet in private with your "enemy," with restoration to fellowship as the goal.

Unfortunately, most of us have never read Jesus' procedure for restoring the person who has sinned—or we disregard it. We much prefer to get on the telephone and voice a prayer concern about someone who has sinned (especially if it is against us and our sensibilities). Or we express our concern at prayer meetings, for we are sure that the sanctuary will sanctify our gossip. Or else we use prayers as a substitute for obedience, for going "in private" to the person who has sinned.

"But," you say, "I know I can forgive. I can even welcome that person into my circle of fellowship, but I cannot and will not *forget*. Don't get me involved in any project that would force me to work closely with that person, for I do not want to get hurt again. I want to protect myself from repeatedly getting hurt."

Beware of that attitude. That is not biblical forgiveness. True biblical forgiveness says, "I am willing to restore, to gain, to win my brother and sister." You see, that is the way God treated us when we came to Him in repentance and faith. He forgave us our sin and said, "I will remember it no more." (See Heb. 8:12.)

At this point you are probably thinking, *OK, I'll grant you that the goal of forgiveness is reconciliation. But do you understand what this is going to cost me?*

Yes, I do, for Jesus illustrated that as well in Matthew 18:23-35. Peter asked, "Lord, how often shall my brother sin against me and I forgive him? Up to seven times?" I sense that in that question Peter was trying to deal with restoring the sinning brother or sister. And in his mind he was saying, *Lord, you are really letting those sinning people get off easily. I go to the person who has wronged me, show him his sin in love and forgiveness, and he promptly admits his sin. I know human nature, and it won't be long and he will wrong me again. So I go back and am able to restore him again. Off he goes on his way—and two weeks later he has cheated me again. How long can this go on?*

The rabbis had taught that you forgive a person three times. Peter went for the biblical number, seven. He expected to be congratulated for his magnanimity. So when Jesus said, "I do not say to you, up to seven times," Peter was thinking, *See, I was too high.* He could not believe his ears when Jesus continued, "but up to seventy times seven" (v. 22). Peter's mental calculator lit up and numbers started flashing, settling on 490. Mind-boggling! You might as well say "a zillion times." For in reality, Jesus was saying that forgiveness must be unlimited.

The Cost of Forgiveness

To help Peter and the others present to understand the cost of this kind of forgiveness, Jesus told the Parable of the Wealthy King who had his annual accounting of receivables, of debts owed him. In the lineup was an absolutely terrified debtor who would rather face an angry wife than the king, for his debt had become so large that he could not possibly repay it. The king looked at the sum the man owed him and thundered, in effect, "You scoundrel. You've taken advantage of my generosity long enough." Turning to his treasurer, he said, "Sell him, his wife, and his children on the slave market. We'll get what we can. At least then his debt won't increase next year."

The man thought of his lovely wife and beautiful children and threw himself at the feet of the king, saying, "I realize I have not done right by you. Give me some time and I really will repay everything I owe you."

The king looked down at the groveling debtor for a long minute and then said, "I ought to have my head examined, but I will let you go free this time. You will not need to go to auction on the slave market. I am forgiving you all your indebtedness for the sake of your wife and children."

I suspect the man did not even stop for a cup of coffee on his way home. He burst into the house and shouted, "We're free! The king has forgiven us all our indebtedness. We are free!" He may even have gone on to the neighbors to tell of the king's generosity.

Jesus told this story for the sake of Peter and the disciples—and all those who would some day read it in the Bible. The wealthy king is God. We have, in effect, all stood before God's judgment bar and heard Him say "You owe Me an infinite amount of righteousness, for that is what I require of man." And not one of us could pay it. No matter how hard we try, we will not impress God with our goodness. So God, through the death of Jesus Christ, freely forgave our sins.

The king freely forgave his debtor, just as God has freely forgiven us. That makes forgiveness free, does it not? Wrong. Forgiveness is never free. True, from the standpoint of the debtor, the forgiveness of his debt was free. From our standpoint as believers, the forgiveness of our sin was free. In both cases, however, the cost was great. Let it be written in mile-high letters: *The cost of forgiveness is great. The cost of reconciliation is immeasurable.*

In the parable, the king absorbed the cost. He had to make a huge bad-debt entry, a $10 million write-off in today's dollars. It cost him a major chunk of his fortune to forgive the debtor.

Even so, God gives forgiveness freely to repentant sinners, but that does not make it cheap. God absorbed the debt of our sins when Jesus died on the cross in our place. He payed His own justice its due.

How does this apply when we forgive one another? The point to remember is that the score always has to be evened. Here's a man who commits adultery and his wife forgives him. How is that score evened? She absorbs the loss when she forgives her husband. The one who is sinned against bears in her own body, in her emotions and spirit, the brunt of the sin committed against her. Because that is the case, she has the right and the ability to do as the king did, forgive.

Is that right? Let me ask you another question. Is it right that Jesus Christ died on the cross, taking in His own body the penalty for our sins, the penalty we deserved? Paul spoke to that when he wrote, "And be kind one to another, tenderhearted, forgiving each other, just as God in Christ also has forgiven you" (Eph. 4:32). Once we see that our standard of forgiveness is set by the forgiveness Jesus extended to us by dying in our place, we can understand why we must forgive our brothers or sisters so many times. We recognize that the debt is paid through the hurt we bear when we forgive the other person freely—just as Christ forgave us.

But you say, "I just am not ready to bear that cost. There is too much at stake now. I will forgive later when I am in a better position emotionally to bear the cost." Take another look at the cost of unforgiveness in Jesus' parable. Notice that the debtor who had been completely forgiven went out after he had finished his rejoicing and demanded instant payment from someone who owed him a small amount. It was the size of debt you might owe a friend because your money ran out on a trip and you borrowed $20. Instead of having mercy on his debtor, the forgiven man threw his friend in prison until he could pay back the $20 he owed.

In those days there was no legal aid, so the man in prison was without recourse at law. Nor did the police permit him the one mandatory telephone call U.S. law demands. His friends had to take action on his behalf (fortunate the man who has friends like that). They notified the king of this ungrateful act. The king then summoned the man whom he had previously forgiven and asked: "You wicked slave, I forgave you all that debt because you entreated me. Should you not also have had mercy on your fellow slave, even as I had mercy on you?" (Matt. 18:32-33) And the king handed the man over to the torturers until he would repay that which he had once been forgiven!

What If I Don't Forgive

End of story? No, for Jesus then emphasized the cost of bitterness, anger, and an *unforgiving* spirit by saying, "So shall My heavenly Father also do to you, if each of you does not forgive his brother from your heart" (v. 35).

Let's be specific. You may go to church Sunday morning, knowing you have not given God the time He deserved during the week. It is communion Sunday and you know you cannot take the bread and the cup with that between you and God. So you confess it and are forgiven. Then as you walk toward your car, you see a business associate who took advantage of your absence during vacation to ingratiate himself with the boss. You start telling your family about it for the hundredth time and say, "I hope God gets him for that!"

What is the cost of your *un*forgiveness? The immediate cost may be the loss of respect in your family (usually not expressed, but it happens just the same). Another cost is personal stress. The real cost is that expressed by Jesus: "So shall My heavenly Father also do to you, if each of you does not forgive his brother from your heart" (v. 35). We should not interpret this verse to mean that God revokes our forgiveness if we don't forgive others. But He does promise us torment if we withhold forgiveness from *anyone* who has wronged us.

Years ago my pastor's wife made a statement that is so true here: "Forgiveness is something good that you do for yourself." In other words, forgiving someone else has the benefit of restoring that person. But you benefit as well, because if you maintain that bitterness it will cloud your spirit and your relationships with everyone around you—and you will be cast into the emotional torture that is inevitable if you do not forgive.

You say, "OK, I recognize that the goal of forgiveness is reconciliation. I am aware of the cost to God of forgiving my sins, and I know what it will cost me if I forgive the person who has wronged me. I'll admit as well the emotional cost of unforgiveness. But how do I get myself to forgive? I don't feel a bit like forgiving anyone."

That last sentence is at the root of most unforgiving attitudes. We have been taught that our feelings are important, that they are the motivators to action. If we do not *feel* like doing something, we should not do it. Some go so far as to say that until you feel like doing it, the Holy Spirit is not guiding you.

Take another look at Matthew 18:35. Then go back and read verses 21-22. Do you find anything about the need to *feel* like forgiving anyone? Jesus clearly and unequivocally gave a command. We are to forgive our brothers or sisters an unlimited number of times, *no matter how little we feel like doing it*. Amazingly, feelings always follow obedience, even if they may lag a bit because our emotional makeup is sluggish.

You may be one of those who has been rejected by your parents. In your heart you are saying, and you may well be saying it to your spouse, "I want to see my parents suffer for what they have done to me. No way am I going to let them off scot-free by forgiving them." You say that even though in your most honest hours you admit they couldn't care less about whether you forgave them or not. They have rejected you—and they will continue to reject you. Your clear response, if you want to live by God's Word, must be, "By God's grace, I choose to forgive them. I choose to forgive them for all the hurt they have caused me." That will, I can assure you, take you out of the torture chamber of bitterness, anger, and resentment.

Why do I say that? I say it not only because I know it is psychologically sound, but because it is biblically sound as well. Christ taught that we have the power to bind anything on earth or loose it; He said that if two of us agree on earth about anything, it shall be done; and these promises apply directly to the acts of reconciliation and forgiveness. Special help is available when we forgive another and when believers are reconciled. That's why those promises appear right in the middle of Christ's discussion of forgiveness (vv. 18-20).

There are marriages across this land that are bound because there has been no loving confrontation and reconciliation. There are families in which the Spirit of God is not free to work because of unforgiving attitudes. Churches are bound, unable to glorify God, because of irreconcilable factions in the church. The Lord wants to set you and me free through honest, loving confrontation, forgiveness, and restoration.

Some years ago a revival swept through western Canada and into parts of the United States. One of the events that sparked it happened in a Baptist church in Saskatoon, Saskatchewan. In that church, two brothers had not spoken to each other for 13 years. They would enter and leave the church sanctuary through different doors. Both had long ago given up on prayer. The pastor, who was one of the few who knew about the feud, said to them during the early days of the revival, "I'm going to bring both of you down to the basement, and we as deacons are going to gather around you. We are not letting you go until you are reconciled. Take as much time as you want, but we are going to be praying and asking God to bring peace into this situation."

So the pressure was on. Finally, one brother said to the other, "OK, I want you to forgive me for all the wrong that I've done."

And the other responded, "Well, it's about time. It's about time you see that you are at fault in this whole business."

The pastor and the deacons just kept on praying. Others joined in as the deacons said, "God, this isn't good enough. We've got to get a genuine reconciliation." Well, the Holy Spirit of God came into that circle and took those two men apart, piece by piece. One of the people in the auditorium said he heard the man with the haughty spirit eventually pound the downstairs wall for 20 minutes, asking God to forgive him, repenting of the bitterness that had been built up in him. The next evening, those two brothers sang a duet in that church. It was from that atmosphere, that kind of loosing of bound spirits, that the revival spread through hundreds of churches. All over the land, believers met in loving confrontation as families were reconciled, people in churches were reconciled, and the many hurts of life were healed.

How do you tackle a bitter, unforgiving spirit within yourself? You go in obedience to Christ, regardless of how you feel, and tell the one who has hurt you that you forgive him or her. You do it by faith in the Christ who died for you and forgave your sin. And if you do not get a response? Then just like Jesus, you wait until that person's heart is opened to your loving forgiveness.

Let's etch the words of Paul on our minds: "And be kind to one another, tenderhearted, forgiving each other, just as God in Christ also has forgiven you" (Eph. 4:32).

If you've got someone to forgive, do it *now*.

Application

1. Name the one person or organization that you feel most bitter toward. List the reasons why you think you

have every right to feel bitter.

2. Now list the reasons why God should be displeased with you on the basis of your actions during your adult years.

3. Read what God has done for you in the light of the things listed in number 2 (Rom. 5:1-8; Eph. 1:3-7; 1 Peter 2:24).

4. How are we to treat those who genuinely mistreat us, according to Jesus? (Matt. 5:44)

5. Consider creative ways in which you can do good to those who have caused bitterness in your heart. Take the first step today to begin implementing that plan of action.

12

Living with Sorrow

ONE spring day, a car with four young people skidded on an icy stretch of pavement in Canada. The 18-year-old driver swerved to the opposite ditch, hoping to miss an oncoming truck. But unfortunately, he was only partially successful. His own life was spared, but the two young people in the backseat and a young mother in the front were killed instantly.

One of those young people killed was my nephew, whose name was Dallas. He was my brother's oldest child, his only son. He was the first member of our immediate family to die. Though I had attended scores of funerals in my lifetime, this one was different. Death had struck close to home. Sorrow, that deep sense of pain and loss, became ours by personal experience.

Our world is filled with sorrow. The wife of a friend of mine chose to file for divorce recently. For Joe, his wife's action was as intense as if she had died. If she had died, he would have accepted the loss more easily than he had the divorce. His loneliness was compounded by extreme feelings of regret, mixed with generous doses of anger and bitterness. Reading the Bible seemed impossible, prayer futile.

Consider also the sorrow experienced by families who have to move every two or three years because the head office says so. After months of house-hunting, they find exactly the kind of neighborhood in which their children can be raised. The children start off to school, eventually make friends, and develop relationships with the children in the neighborhood. Mother starts volunteer work at the hospital, serves with a women's group at church, and enters into significant friendships with several women. Then the husband is told, "Now if you want a promotion, you will have to move to yet another city." The sorrow that this family experiences from the breakup of relationships can be traumatic for most members, for they know that in all likelihood they will never make contact with their friends again.

However, sorrow is not necessarily bad. In fact, it can be beneficial if handled properly. It can be God's way of causing us to enter another phase of our lives, a time that will have its own benefits. Yet improperly handled, sorrow can be devastating. Sorrow can lock people into a total preoccupation with past relationships and events and thus prevent growth.

Think of the widow of a well-liked professor who had built up a considerable library before he died. Determined to maintain the memory of her late husband, the widow insists that his library be left intact. No one can come to use the books, nor can the books be given away. That would be disloyal to the memory of her husband. As a result, she never reenters life the way God expects her to; she stays home, bogged down with memories.

Then there is the person loaded down with a tremendous amount of guilt. He takes responsibility for things that may have contributed to the death of a loved one. I remember visiting the home of a widow whose husband had died of a heart attack years ago. Over and over she said, "If he had only been persuaded to see a doctor. I told him he ought to go, but maybe if I had been more persistent he would have gone." That kind of guilt leads to a neurotic preoccupation with "if only" and is not pleasing to God. As human beings, we are subject to all kinds of frailties and we make many mistakes. But God does not expect us to live with the guilt caused by our weaknesses. We are not omniscient; only God is.

I believe that we can learn how to mourn in a profitable way, how to reenter life after tragedy, from the life of Jesus Christ. His example gives us clues to how we can and should respond to sorrow. Isaiah told us that He was "a man of sorrows, and acquainted with grief" (Isa. 53:3). We will examine several situations in which grief touched Him.

As I considered Jesus' response to tragedy, I asked myself, *How did Jesus respond when His cousin, John the Baptist, was brutally murdered?* Their mothers had been good friends, so there is reason to believe that John and Jesus knew each other well before that public baptism at Jordan. Now this preacher of righteousness, the forerunner of the Messiah, had fallen victim to the vicious hatred of Herod's wife, Herodias. At the request of this woman's daughter, John the Baptist's head had been carried in on a platter in a gruesome display of vindictiveness.

A Few Moments Alone

Matthew reported that "his disciples came and took away the body and buried it; and they went and reported to Jesus" (Matt. 14:12). Our Lord's reaction is reported in verse 13: "Now when Jesus heard it, He withdrew from there in a boat, to a lonely place by Himself." Jesus' action illustrates the first principle in living with sorrow: *He withdrew to a lonely place.* True, He later requested the help of His friends, but for the time being He needed to be alone.

Like Jesus, there are times when our thoughts are so private, our sorrows so intense and our hurts so deep, that we need to get alone with God and pour out our complaints to Him. For one thing, we need to be alone to meditate. A time of sorrow presents an opportunity to reflect upon the past, to evaluate our lives, to distinguish what is important from what is unimportant. At such a time we begin to ask, "God, as I consider my frailty, what do You want me to do?" This time of meditation can lead to significant new beginnings if we do not stay with the past.

Furthermore, our times alone should be spent in prayer. That is actually what Jesus intended to do, but the multitudes heard of His retreat and barged in on Him. In fact, their presence led directly to the feeding of the 5,000. But when that was over, "immediately He made the disciples get into the boat, and go ahead of Him to the other side. . . . And after He had sent the multitudes away, He went up to the mountain by Himself to pray; and when it was evening, He was there alone" (vv. 22-23).

It is in the quietness of our souls that we ought to pour out our hearts before God. There may be times when we are upset and even angry, but we ought to be honest with the Lord God. Read the story of David in Psalm 77. In effect David was saying, "I pour out my complaint to You, God. Is it going to be this way forever? Are You never going to listen to me? Are You never going to be concerned about me again?" In words like that, David unleashed the agony of his spirit before God. Today we also need times like that when we are honest with God, when we pour out our frustrations and desires in our sorrow

Resume Normal Activities
Yet Jesus did not stay alone. He kept life in balance, as we need to, and resumed normal activities. He went from a time alone to feeding the 5,000. Then, after another time alone He went to the disciples, walking to

them on the water as they were afraid of capsizing in the storm. He went from His need to their need. That is the second principle: *We must resume the normal activities of life.*

You and I have both seen instances when after a funeral, loved ones and friends come in and do everything for the grieving survivor. "Now just lie down; we want you to do nothing," they may say to the mother who has lost a son. "We will scrub your floors, do your dishes." Yet this expression of Christian love poses a problem, if overdone. The person beset by sorrow may develop an unrealistic picture of life and may have difficulty reentering life to make those common, everyday decisions so necessary to living with sorrow.

One of the most important things you can do in a time of sorrow is to continue, as much as possible, the normal activities that force you to make decisions. This will help you orient yourself to your new life without the loved one. Even if you do not have to go to work on a job, it is important to keep up activities at home that will move you forward. Inactivity lets you dwell too much on the tragedy. That's why Jesus resumed His regular schedule.

The story of David in the Old Testament contains a striking example illustrating this principle. When Absalom his son had been killed by Joab after an intense battle won by David's army, David went to an upper chamber and wept. Hadn't he given the command that Absalom's life was to be spared despite his rebellion? Now Absalom was dead, and David was overcome with grief.

When Joab was told, "Behold, the king is weeping and mourns for Absalom" (2 Sam. 19:1), he went to David and said in effect, "David, don't you realize that your mourning is going to create real problems for you? The people have won a great victory, and you are overcome by sorrow. If you don't snap out of it and join the victory celebrations, the soldiers will go home. Your mourning is simply unrealistic in the light of what was accomplished by your people." Though David was personally deeply grieved by the death of his son, he needed to reenter life and resume his normal kingly duties if he was to hold the respect of his people.

Like David, we need to cope with our sorrow by thinking of the needs of others. Jesus also provides us with an example in John 13. He knew He was about to die, and already this must have caused some inner heaviness. Yet He rose from supper, took a towel, and poured water to start washing the disciples' feet. Even though He knew what was coming, He thought of others.

Nothing will help you overcome sorrow like asking, "How can I get involved in the needs of others?" The moment you start thinking and acting like that, you will discover people with far greater needs than yours. I can personally testify to this, that no matter how tragic our situation may be, there are situations even more tragic. This helps to provide balance to our experiences and makes it easier to live with sorrow.

Accept Sorrow As a Phase of Transition

A third principle that I find in the life of Christ is that *there is a time to mourn and a time to be joyful*. The disciples of John came to Jesus and asked, "Why do we and the Pharisees fast, but Your disciples do not fast?" (Matt. 9:14) And Jesus replied that while the Bridegroom is present, it is time to rejoice, but when He is absent they will mourn. And in John 16:20-21 Jesus said, "You will weep and lament, but the world will rejoice; you will be sorrowful, but your sorrow will be turned to joy. Whenever a woman is in travail she has sorrow, because her hour has come; but when she gives birth to the child, she remembers the anguish no more, for joy that a child has been born into the world." Jesus was in effect reiterating what Ecclesiastes says: There is a time to mourn, but there also is a time to laugh (Ecc. 3:4). In other words, everything has its time—and sorrow has its time too.

We might benefit by reinstating an Old Testament practice, that of allowing a certain period of mourning for the dead. It was an excellent idea from the psychological viewpoint. For 40 days after a person died, his family would mourn, and then life resumed its normal pattern. In no way do I suggest that you can forget the loved one in 40 days. You cannot and you never will. But it *does* mean that you realize that it is unrealistic to spend your whole life in mourning. There is a time to mourn, but there is also a time to rejoice.

Years ago in Europe and in some ethnic communities in the United States, people used to wear black armbands for perhaps three months after a loved one died. This was a sign that the members of the family were mourning. I think that was a healthy thing to do— to recognize that there are times when we mourn and there are times when we rejoice, to see it as a phase of life rather than the normal experience for the rest of our lives. Then mourning becomes a period of development and change, rather than an endless process that we take with us to the grave.

Share Your Grief with Others

In sorrow Christ also *requested the help of friends.* This time we see Jesus in Gethsemane. He had come to the garden with His disciples and asked them to pray for Him. He took Peter, James, and John with Him "and began to be grieved and distressed" (Matt. 26:37). I don't know how much of this was visible to the three disciples, but they certainly should have understood the implicit call for help when He said to them, "My soul is deeply grieved, to the point of death; remain here and keep watch with Me" (v. 38).

The amazing thing is that though the disciples were

not very good at encouraging the Lord in His final night of agony, He did not consider it beneath His dignity to ask for their help and prayer support. Sometimes we think that someone as strong as Jesus, or a friend we know, really does not need that support. But Jesus did. And if Jesus needed it, how much more do we need it in our hour of grief?

You say, "I don't have close friends like that." Then call someone you do not know as well. He may well become your closest friend as a result of joining in your sorrow in prayer. Simply say to that person, "I am going to ask you to stand with me during this time of personal grief. I want you to pray with me, and for me, and uphold me in a ministry of encouragement during this time." God gives us friends for times like this; that's what the body of Christ, the local church, is all about.

Accept Tragedy As the Will of God

I see a fifth principle in the life of Jesus. *He accepted tragedy as the will of God.* We read, "The Son of man is to go, just as it is written of Him" (Matt. 26:24). Jesus was saying that His death was not an accident. It was part of a divine plan, and He accepted it as such. They could not take Him until His hour was come.

We too must accept tragedy as part of God's divine plan. We are continually saying, "What *if* we had called the doctor sooner. *If* he had operated, the person would have lived." We get so bogged down in the "what if's" of life because we have never really accepted the tragedy as part of the divine plan. We act as if life depends on us, as if it is our responsibility if someone dies. Yet if we are acting on the basis of information available to us and somehow make a wrong decision, we must accept our loved one's death as the will of God. If not, we become overloaded with guilt and may be emotionally crippled for the rest of our lives.

Consider this fact: Jesus, as the Son of God, could

have prevented the death of John the Baptist. He could have spoken the word, and John would have lived and Herod died instead. Jesus had all that power in His fingers, by the word of His mouth. He didn't use it, yet He did not live with guilt, either, or a neurotic preoccupation with the tragic death of His cousin. He accepted the total picture as the will of God. John the Baptist's death was as much a part of God's plan as was the death of Christ.

There are cases of reasonable guilt. You may have had a bad relationship with the person who died. You may have mistreated that person. If so, you must realize that there is forgiveness for your sin. We read in 1 John 1:9: "If we confess our sins, He is faithful and righteous to forgive us our sins and to cleanse us from all unrighteousness." That commitment by God includes all of those wrong decisions, misjudgments, and sins in your life. God wants you to be free so that you might have confidence in Him, so that you might bow humbly and accept the situation as from His hand even though you bear responsibility. When you confess it, it is blotted out as far as your relationship with God is concerned. God wants you to be released from guilt through His forgiveness.

Lay Aside Resentment
Notice also that *Christ bore no resentment*. When Jesus was on the cross, He said, "Father, forgive them; for they do not know what they are doing" (Luke 23:34). That's the sixth lesson we can learn from Him. We need to be reminded of this because at no time are we more critical than at the time of a tragedy.

I pity doctors. When a patient dies, they get blamed for having operated, and if they did not operate, they get blamed for that. We sometimes expect people in the medical profession to play God, to know precisely how the treatment is going to work out. If it does not work

out the way we think it should, we hold them account-
able. We get very critical of anyone and anything associated with the death of a loved one.

Jesus could have been critical too. He could have said,
"I have done no wrong; I am sinless." He could have
thought to Himself, *Why is it that I am being unjustly pun-
ished and bearing the sins of the world? On top of that, I am
being accused of things I didn't do.* Yet Jesus bore no resentment. He died with a spirit free of anger, hatred, and
retaliation.

Jesus gave us a clue to what our attitude is to be toward sorrow when He said, "Blessed are those who
mourn, for they shall be comforted" (Matt. 5:4). As we
accept our griefs, our sorrows can be used of God to
develop within us the ability to comfort others.

When I flew to Canada for the funeral of my nephew,
my brother and I discussed all the "if's" by which the
accident might have been avoided. If only they had been
going a little slower, if only they had started out a little
earlier—if, if. You can easily come up with a hundred
if's. But I was so pleased when my brother said to me,
"You know, if what you wrote in one of your books was
right, it means that we have to accept this as the will of
God without all the if's." And I think that is how God
wants us to respond to tragedy.

This does not mean that we do not sorrow. Jesus wept
openly at the grave of Lazarus (John 11:35). But as Christians, we must ultimately accept sorrow as part of the
fabric of life. If we let sorrow tie us to the past, we will
never experience life as Jesus wants us to. There is a time
to cry, there is a time to dance, there is a time to weep,
and there is a time to laugh. We can do it as we respond
positively to what God lets enter our lives.

Sorrow Is Temporary
Finally, *Christ believed our sorrow was only temporary.*
That's why He told His disciples, "Let not your heart be

troubled" (John 14:1). He was leaving to prepare a place for them, "And if I go and prepare a place for you, I will come again, and receive you to Myself; that where I am, there you may be also" (v. 3). Read the description of heaven in the Book of Revelation and you'll be convinced with the Apostle Paul that "the sufferings of this present time are not worthy to be compared with the glory that is to be revealed to us" (Rom. 8:18).

Remember that when a believer dies, we do not sorrow for him. In the last analysis, grief is for ourselves. A part of us is gone, but our loved one is with the Lord, which is "far better."

Believers have the assurance that their sorrow will indeed be turned into joy. Christ taught, "Blessed are those who mourn, for they shall be comforted" (Matt. 5:4).

Application

1. Study John 11:1-40 as an example of sorrow. The fact of Christ's special love for Martha, Mary, and Lazarus did not exempt them from heartbreak. Why did Christ wait before returning to Bethany? (v. 6) Why could Christ say He was glad despite the sorrow of the family? (v. 15) What words of comfort did Christ speak to those who mourned? (vv. 25-26) What does Christ's own response tell us about His identification with human need?

2. Read Revelation 21:1-7. How will the emotion of sorrow be resolved in heaven?

3. Discuss: When is sorrow normal and healthy? When does it become abnormal and destructive?

Other Books by Erwin Lutzer:

How to Say No to a Stubborn Habit
Every day you face the oldest human dilemma—the choice between good and evil. The good news is that you can say No to sin and Yes to God.

Living with Your Passions
Sexual passions have a way of demanding immediate attention. This book tells how God-given grace and power will help you deal with your sexual desires.

When a Good Man Falls
Can a Christian hope to become effective again after being tripped up by sin? Discover how to make a comeback—or how to help a loved one recover from seeming ruin.

Dear Reader:

We would like to know your opinion of **Managing Your Emotions**
Your ideas will help us as we strive to continue offering books that will
satisfy your needs and interests.

Send your responses to:

VICTOR BOOKS
1825 College Avenue
Wheaton, IL 60187

What most influenced your decision to purchase this book?
- ☐ Front cover
- ☐ Title
- ☐ Author
- ☐ Back cover material
- ☐ Price
- ☐ Length
- ☐ Subject
- ☐ Other:_____

What did you like about this book?
- ☐ Good reference tool
- ☐ Helped me understand myself better
- ☐ Helped me understand others better
- ☐ Helped me understand the Bible
- ☐ Helped me understand God
- ☐ It was easy to teach
- ☐ Author

How was this book used?
- ☐ For my personal reading
- ☐ Studied it in a group situation
- ☐ Used it to teach a group
- ☐ As a reference tool
- ☐ For a church or school library

If you used this book to teach a group, did you also use the accompanying leader's guide? ☐ YES ☐ NO

Please indicate your level of interest in reading other Victor books like this one.
- ☐ Very interested
- ☐ Somewhat interested
- ☐ Not very interested
- ☐ Not at all interested

Would you recommend this book to a friend?   ☐ YES   ☐ NO

Please indicate your age.
   ☐ Under 18   ☐ 25-34   ☐ 45-54
   ☐ 18-24   ☐ 35-44   ☐ 55 or over

Would you like to receive more information about Victor books? If so, please fill in your name and address:

NAME:_____

ADDRESS:_____

_____

Do you have additional comments or suggestions regarding Victor books?